What Your Colleagues A

"*Worthwhile, intentional,* and *thorough* are watchwords to [...] and Frey's *Rigorous Reading.* This book provides teachers and teacher-leaders with the critical information they need to unfold Florida's B.E.S.T. Standards and improve transdisciplinary literacy acquisition across grade levels. It is mindfully written for those closest to the students— the classroom teachers."

—ENRIQUE A. PUIG, EdD
Director, Morgridge International Reading Center
University of Central Florida

"Fisher and Frey have truly outdone themselves with this must-read for all Florida educators— preservice to secondary. *Rigorous Reading* effortlessly moves from theory to practice while explicitly addressing necessary scaffolds to ensure *each and every* student can access complex text. The five access points are exactly what educators need to elevate learning and increase cognitive engagement through strong literacy instruction."

—COURTNEY LOUGH
Senior Instructional Specialist, ELA K–6
Pasco County Schools, FL

"Just as our students require scaffolded instruction, so do we teachers in an ever-changing educational landscape. In this book, Fisher and Frey offer Florida's teachers the *what* and the *how* of providing the nuts and bolts to students with diverse needs and states of readiness."

—PAUL HOLIMON
Instructional Coach, Collier County Public Schools, Naples, FL
Past-President, Florida's Council of Language Arts Supervisors

"This is a bold book. . . . It is genius, and its unique contribution is in bringing the balance and the centeredness to new education standards."

—P. DAVID PEARSON
University of California, Berkeley

"With *Rigorous Reading*, Doug Fisher and Nancy Frey have provided literacy educators who are committed to successfully raising the bar with solutions that make sense. The book is masterfully developed with an extensive reach across many grade levels in terms of defining what it means to provide intentional instruction and teaching text complexity. The five access points are discussed pragmatically with evidence of a solid research base deftly woven throughout the book. This is the most practical book I have come across in terms of providing teachers with the knowledge base and assistance many are seeking to improve their instruction with regard to complex texts."

—STEVEN L. LAYNE, EdD
Author of *Igniting a Passion for Reading*

"In *Rigorous Reading: 5 Access Points for Comprehending Complex Texts*, Fisher and Frey help teachers understand how to bring vigor to rigor. They teach us how to help students understand more from their complex texts—greater understanding that will help to bring life and energy to each student's reading. Rooted in solid research, this is book is a must-read for those grappling with how to translate the recommendations and mandates around text complexity into instructional practices."

—JENNIFER SERRAVALLO
Author of *Teaching Reading in Small Groups* and
Conferring With Readers

"[W]e need resources that show us how to support students in developing their full literacy potential. In this very practical and insightful book, Fisher and Frey examine how conceptions of text complexity are causing us to shift some of our ideas about reading instruction. *Rigorous Reading* is an important resource that will help teachers align reading instruction in powerful ways."

—LINDA B. GAMBRELL
Professor, Clemson University

RIGOROUS READING

FLORIDA EDITION

RIGOROUS READING

NOW WITH FLORIDA'S B.E.S.T. STANDARDS!

5 Access Points for Comprehending Complex Texts

FLORIDA EDITION

DOUGLAS FISHER

NANCY FREY

FOREWORD BY EUGENE PRINGLE, JR.

CORWIN
Fisher & Frey

FOR INFORMATION:

Corwin

A SAGE Company

2455 Teller Road

Thousand Oaks, California 91320

(800) 233-9936

www.corwin.com

SAGE Publications Ltd.

1 Oliver's Yard

55 City Road

London EC1Y 1SP

United Kingdom

SAGE Publications India Pvt. Ltd.

B 1/I 1 Mohan Cooperative Industrial Area

Mathura Road, New Delhi 110 044

India

SAGE Publications Asia-Pacific Pte. Ltd.

18 Cross Street #10-10/11/12

China Square Central

Singapore 048423

Director and Publisher, Corwin Classroom: Lisa Luedeke

Editorial Development Manager: Julie Nemer

Associate Content Development Editor: Sharon Wu

Production Editor: Melanie Birdsall

Copy Editor: Sarah J. Duffy

Typesetter: C&M Digitals (P) Ltd.

Proofreader: Theresa Kay

Indexer: Integra

Cover Designer: Janet Kiesel

Marketing Manager: Deena Meyer

Printed in Canada

ISBN 978-1-0718-1063-7

Library of Congress Control Number: 2020909113

This book is printed on acid-free paper.

20 21 22 23 24 10 9 8 7 6 5 4 3 2 1

Contents

CHAPTER 6. Access Point Five: Assessing Students' Understanding

Visit the companion website at
resources.corwin.com/rigorousreadingfla
for access to video clips and other resources.

■ ■ ■

Note From the Publisher: *The authors have provided video and web content throughout the book that is available to you through QR (quick response) codes. To read a QR code, you must have a smartphone or tablet with a camera. We recommend that you download a QR code reader app that is made specifically for your phone or tablet brand.*

List of Videos

Access the following videos at **resources.corwin.com/rigorousreadingfla**.

Chapter 1

Video 1.1 Doug discusses text complexity.
Video 1.2 Doug discusses close reading.
Video 1.3 Doug talks about the gradual release of responsibility.

Chapter 2

Video 2.1 Teacher models comprehension strategies.
Video 2.2 Teacher models for her students.
Video 2.3 Elementary teacher models word solving.
Video 2.4 High school teacher models word solving.
Video 2.5 Making learning visible through learning intentions.

Chapter 3

Video 3.1 Close reading with sixth-grade English language learners.
Video 3.2 Student rereads and discusses a complex text in high school English.
Video 3.3 Close reading of historical information.
Video 3.4 Close reading and text-dependent questions in upper elementary school.
Video 3.5 Close reading in the primary grades.
Video 3.6 Teacher works with groups of students to facilitate their understanding.
Video 3.7 Teacher uses prompts and cues to guide learning.
Video 3.8 Teacher uses questioning techniques to aid student comprehension.
Video 3.9 Teacher works with small groups of students to generate questions.

Chapter 4

Chapter 5

Chapter 6

Foreword

What has remained constant during my time as a Florida educator are the metrics of student success measured through various modes of state accountability.

What has remained constant during my time as a Florida educator is the urgency for teachers to use research-based practices to provide the best quality instruction to students.

What has remained constant during my time as a Florida educator is the push for equitable literacy for all students.

Among the consistencies in principle, concept, and expectation, each constant has been accompanied by a shift. Such shifts include changes in practice, philosophy, curriculum, and pedagogy.

My novice years as a middle school English teacher and literacy instructional coach in the Florida public school system took me on a journey of multiple educational reformations over the course of a five-year period. That period was painted with the adoption of three sets of state standards, programmatic changes in curriculum and instruction resources, school turnaround efforts, a transition to digital instruction, and professional development to accompany each. Among the transition in state standards was the necessity to effectively implement what was currently in place, while preparing for the "next big push."

Despite the subject area, it is notable that through multiple changes a constant has been the notion that we must effectively engage students in complex texts. No instructional program dictated this need. No administration dictated this need. While student data outcomes determined gaps, trends, and needs related to literacy instruction, there was never a time that there was not a need for literacy instruction that would enable students to comprehend complex texts.

As I read this comprehensive and practical guide to engaging students in the reading of these texts, some of the authors' words struck me. The following quote, and those quoted in the remainder of this foreword, spoke to me as an education practitioner *and* as an adult learner.

"It's really like climbing a staircase."

I like to visualize this staircase as one with a definite starting point, but an indefinite number of steps. The climb represents the varied steps that teachers and students take to engage in the fullness of the reading processes. Never deviating from research-based practices, the authors provide a practical approach to successfully guiding students up this staircase through five access points. The sequence mirrors authentic classroom experience, while providing additional strategies and methods for implementation. *Rigorous Reading* maps the course—a tiering of sorts that mimics the natural flow of good, solid instruction. The five access points follow:

1. Modeling and Learning Intentions
2. Close and Scaffolded Reading Instruction
3. Collaborative Conversations
4. An Independent Reading Staircase
5. Assessing Students' Understanding

There is an evident progression of knowledge as you move up the staircase, and the steps serve as building blocks to navigate through some rugged terrain, and for some students, uncharted territory. In their own way, each step gets at the core of literacy instruction, infused with new and innovative ways of teaching and learning.

It was during my second or third year of teaching English when I started to make meaningful connections to each of these access points in some way. While I was an effective teacher, I had not yet woven all these elements together. Struggling internally with my personal gaps when delivering literacy instruction, I vividly recall sitting with my literacy coach and how she explained to me the importance of each of these steps. It was then that I was able to think more critically about how I delivered instruction and the implications of that for my students. The light bulb had gone off and it changed the way I approached teaching my middle school students and adult learners. The authors of this book set the stage for such instruction through an approach that is strategic, meaningful, and well supported.

As you read this book, think about the experiences of students in your own classroom and how these access points apply to them. What are their feelings about reading and writing? Are they engaged in meaningful independent reading practices? How are you scaffolding instruction to meet the individual needs of students? And—are you equipped to address these gaps if they exist? There is no one size fits all approach. However, what is provided in *Rigorous Reading* is a starting point that literacy educators can use to tackle such issues as they arise.

As noted, the access points represent the foundation of engaging students in complex texts; this special Florida edition of *Rigorous Reading* includes guidance on navigating those access points through and with the B.E.S.T. standards.

"Students deserve, at some point in every lesson, to experience the curriculum from the expert's perspective."

Fisher and Frey are the undisputed experts in this field. As Florida transitions to the B.E.S.T. standards, it is vitally important to be grounded in sound and accurate research around the subject matter. As a literacy instructional coach, it was my duty to stay abreast of the most current research-based trends in literacy instruction and provide a means to translate that research to the teachers that I supported so that they could better reach students. Collaboratively, we engaged and made meaning of what was presented to us. In their work, Douglas Fisher and Nancy Frey presented to us the perfect combination of research-based strategies and what those strategies look like in the classroom. It is the guidance of experts like Fisher and Frey that continues to propel individuals to their highest potential.

"As literacy educators you have to ensure that students are engaged in texts that are worthy of their time."

This book is worthy of our time. The implementation of the B.E.S.T. standards is another opportunity to move the needle for students and teachers alike. In order to move the needle forward we must be engaged in practices that will do so. Fisher and Frey put student outcomes at the forefront of this work. Through videos and vignettes, literacy educators can see ourselves in the work. We can see ourselves implementing strategies and practices that have been proven to increase student achievement. Ultimately, we can see ourselves shifting and developing a culture that highly supports, nurtures, and advocates for equitable literacy for all!

—Eugene Pringle, Jr.
Assistant Professor, Bethune-Cookman University

Introduction: Your Access Point

Perhaps it was the title that caught your eye: *Rigorous Reading, Florida Edition: 5 Access Points for Comprehending Complex Texts*. There are several phrases embedded in the title, any one of which could have resonated with you.

We chose *Rigorous Reading* because the language of the Florida standards has made it clear that our students are expected to engage regularly with complex texts. A first step toward doing so is in understanding exactly what makes a given text complex. Quantitative and qualitative measures of literary and informational texts are prompting our field to examine more closely the factors that contribute to text complexity. We stand on the shoulders of giants like William S. Gray, Jeanne Chall, Edward Fry, Elfrieda Hiebert, and so many others who have made it their lives' work to help us understand how a text works. In the past, we have been content to leave these determinations up to others. Now, we are ready to assume more responsibility for understanding what the numbers on the book cover mean. We are growing in our ability to perceive the nuances that make some texts more complex than others, especially in divining those qualities that only a knowledgeable human reader can perceive.

But knowing the breadth and depth of a text is not sufficient, and perhaps you picked up this book because the word *Comprehend* captured your attention. That's not surprising—did you know that reading comprehension studies are the oldest in the field of educational research? The earliest use of the term *comprehension* as it relates to reading was by J. Russell Webb in his *Normal Series of School Readers to Teach Correct Reading*, published in 1856. (By the way, the full title also promised to *Improve and Expand the Mind and Purify and Elevate the Character*.) Comprehension is fundamental in reading, and in this book. Without deep understanding, complex texts are inanimate objects. It is only in the reader's mind that a text comes to life. It is truly wondrous that the physical limitations of time and space vanish when a reader engages in silent dialogue with a writer. As teachers of reading, we want to share what Beatrix Potter imagined from her garden in the English countryside. As teachers of literacy in the disciplines, we want to make it possible for Aristotle's formal logic to come to life in the mind of a 21st century adolescent. Maybe J. Russell Webb was right after all.

Chances are good, though, that the phrase *Access Points* was the clincher. The five access points we discuss in this book form its core. It would be woefully inadequate to simply fill a room with complex texts and believe that was enough. If it were, we could simply park our students for a decade or so in the great libraries in our schools and communities. But communing with Potter and Aristotle, not to mention Junot Díaz, Chinua Achebe, Bashō, and Zu Chongzhi, is not possible without granting students access to these ideas. The five access points build a bridge between the reader and the text and are accomplished through intentional instruction:

1. Establishing reasons for reading a complex text, and modeling how an expert reader (you) makes meaning
2. Providing scaffolded and close reading instruction to guide students through complex texts
3. Creating opportunities for collaborative conversations between students to refine their understanding
4. Moving them forward through independent reading of increasingly complex texts
5. Using formative assessment opportunities so you and the reader know what is known, and what is not yet known

We wrote this book with *access* in mind, and our intention is to provide you with a road map for ensuring that all the students you work with, both now and in the future, can come to know what we collectively have known: The world of texts, whether print or digital, represents a history of our past and the promise of our future. Given that imperative, is there anything more important we can do than to open up access for children and adolescents?

Ramping Up for Complex Texts

1

Helping students read more and better has always been the goal of literacy educators. In our profession, we've tried all kinds of approaches to ensure that students can read and understand the wide range of texts they will be confronted with as they grow and develop. There have been times in our history when students were assigned to read hard texts independently. The thinking at the time was that exposure to great works alone would result in learned citizens. That didn't work because students found summaries that they could use to answer comprehension questions and write essays, although it certainly spawned a whole new publishing category: commercial study guides. Doug remembers being assigned to read *Antigone* and searching everywhere for CliffsNotes so that he could complete the required worksheets and write his essay in response to this prompt:

Identify the tragic hero of one of the plays. Analyze the scenes in which the character displays pride and identify the effects that this pride has on the character's life. How could his/her life have been different if he/she had behaved in a less prideful manner?

Thankfully, the answers to this question were clearly articulated in the yellow- and black-striped book. It wasn't that Doug didn't want to read *Antigone*, but rather that although he was assigned to read it, he wasn't taught how to understand an ancient Greek play such that he could answer this prompt. Unfortunately, his teacher did not know that he hadn't read the play because he earned an A on the essay. Lesson learned: Just giving students complex text doesn't mean they will read and understand it.

At other times, we've scaffolded so much that we removed the need for students to read altogether. That didn't work because students were not applying what they had learned to new texts. Nancy remembers a teacher telling her class so much about each assigned chapter of *The Secret Garden* that Nancy didn't feel the need to read the book at all, and Nancy spent her time reading Nancy Drew mysteries instead. She was able to complete all of the tasks (and please her teacher) because the teacher did the majority of the work. The fact that Nancy participated eagerly in classroom discussions wasn't an indication that she was a good reader but rather that she was a good listener. Her teacher's recounting of the previous night's chapter was sufficient for Nancy to engage in rich and collaborative discussions.

Neither of these approaches met the intended goal of getting students to read complex texts. Instead, they relied on either too little, or too much, teaching. To ensure that students actually do learn to read complex texts, teachers have to scaffold instruction and know when to transfer the cognitive and metacognitive responsibility to students. They need to rethink the texts they use, expanding the range to include more complex texts accompanied by scaffolds and support. And they need to carefully consider the intentional instruction students need to receive if they are going to apply what they have learned to the wide world of texts available to them.

In this chapter, we focus on two major concepts in literacy instruction: text complexity and close reading. Given the new Florida B.E.S.T. Standards, you are likely concerned with making it possible for students to read increasingly complex texts and to gain exposure to thoughtful reading instruction that provides access to these texts. Therefore, the first section will address text complexity. The second section will examine the need for students to read these texts closely, critically, and deeply. Starting in kindergarten, text complexity and close and critical reading are important. As the standards note, "Educators should encourage students to wrestle with such complex texts—with proper scaffolding—when they deem it appropriate" (Florida Department of Education, 2020, p. 151). The final portion of the chapter is an introduction to a gradual release of responsibility instructional framework that provides the access points students require to access complex texts.

▶ Reading Complex Texts

Previous standards often included a phrase that required students to read grade-level texts independently. But rarely did standards specify what it meant to have grade-level texts. In 2010, there was widespread acknowledgment that the then current text complexity levels were insufficient to ensure students' success after PK–12 education. In many cases, expectation for students in the PK–12 system topped out at about 1150 Lexile. But college and career success requires that students be able to read much more complex texts than that. Consider the evidence presented by Wei, Cromwell, and McClarty (2016) in their study of text complexity levels of occupational reading materials. They divided occupations into zones based on the level of education provided. For example, Zone 1 required little higher education and included jobs such as food preparation workers, taxi drivers, and food servers. Zone 5, the highest, included jobs for which a master's degree was generally required and included positions such as nutritionist, lawyer, and pharmacist. They collected a variety of texts, such as training guides, reference aids, and handbooks. The average reading level for Zone 1 jobs was grade 11.2 (or about 1300 Lexile), with a high of grade 13.9. Zone 5 jobs averaged at 13.8 (or about 1450 Lexile), with a high of grade 14. In fact, the authors conclude that the average text complexity demands for careers in each job zone are higher than most state standards expect of 9th and 10th graders. In their words, "even jobs that require no formal schooling beyond high school still involve comprehension of texts at the level that should be present at the end of high school," which they identify as a Lexile reading level of between 1150 and 1350.

To ensure that students actually do learn to read complex texts, teachers have to scaffold instruction and know when to transfer the cognitive and metacognitive responsibility to students.

While everyone agrees that we shouldn't just hand students hard texts and wish them well, the practice of scaffolded instruction is receiving renewed attention. How much is too much? When is it not enough?

The new Florida standards that require students to read increasingly complex texts serve as a reminder that the ability to make meaning is the ultimate goal and that carefully crafted instruction on decoding and comprehension is fundamental. The standards also note that students should read multiple genres and text types, both digital and print. We can't imagine any literacy educator disagreeing with either of these parts of the goal. While everyone agrees that teachers shouldn't just hand students hard texts and wish them well, the practice of scaffolded instruction is receiving renewed attention. How much is too much? When is it not enough? There is a deep body of research (e.g., Vygotsky, 1978; Wood, Bruner, & Ross, 1976; Wood & Wood, 1996) on the importance of scaffolding in instruction.

Scaffolded instruction is vital in reading instruction, and its practice is universal. Scaffolding in reading instruction occurs through the use of texts (Fountas & Pinnell, 2012), strategically deployed questions, prompts and cues (Frey & Fisher, 2010), and a gradient of instructional arrangements (Fisher & Frey, 2008; Pearson & Gallagher, 1983). Each of these dimensions of curriculum and instruction is essential for teaching students how to read and for building their capacity to read for meaning. For students to access complex text, their reading experiences must include a thoughtful progression of texts, scaffolds, and instructional arrangements.

A second dimension of the standards concerns exactly what students should be reading. Teachers have operated under tacit agreements about grade level, often relying on local context and traditions. Haven't we all worked in schools where a particular title was considered the province of a specific grade level? For example, where we live, *Charlotte's Web* is third grade, and *Romeo and Juliet* is ninth grade. However, in many cases, these traditions seemed to be justified primarily because units and materials had already been developed and shifting the book to another grade was too much trouble. Given the gap between students' reading levels when they complete high school and the expectations for them when they attend college, the level of text complexity has increased. Teachers must use complex texts that continually stretch students' capacity to read and comprehend literary and informational texts. In other words, the expectation is that students will read and understand more complex texts than they have been expected to in the past. But to what end—and how do we know what makes a text complex?

▶ A New Definition of Text Complexity

In the past, text complexity and readability were viewed interchangeably by many practitioners, even as researchers cautioned otherwise (Hiebert, 2009). Readability has been estimated based on the average length of sentences, the number of syllables in sentences, and—in some cases— occurrences of rare words. These measures provided teachers with general information about readability and were used to gauge appropriate materials for students. But many have voiced concern that these measures missed the nuances present in many texts, often reporting readings as being easier than they really were. Works by Ernest Hemingway, for example, have been assigned a difficulty level ranging from grades 4 to 8, yet any teacher who has used his works of literature knows that the concepts, dialogue, and background knowledge needed by the reader make these texts far more complex than can be measured by a readability formula alone.

Modern definitions of text complexity extend beyond the numeric scores for texts and have been expanded to include qualitative evaluations as well as careful consideration of the reader and tasks. The Florida Standards describe three aspects of text complexity, including:

- **Quantitative aspects,** which include formal readability measures typically conducted by computers
- **Qualitative aspects,** which include levels of meaning, structure, language conventionality and clarity, and knowledge demands typically assessed by human readers
- **Student-centered considerations,** which include students' background knowledge, stamina, and developmental levels as well as the tasks that are assigned to students. (Florida Department of Education, 2020, pp. 148–150)

Text analysis must always keep all three elements in mind.

Quantitative Evaluation

The temptation is to rely on the quantitative measures alone, which are derived from algorithms that yield numerical data; these measures can be calculated by a computer and do an adequate job of tentatively placing a text within a grade band. But these measures alone are inadequate for understanding why one piece of text is qualitatively more

Video 1.1

Doug discusses text complexity.
resources.corwin.com/ rigorousreadingfla

To read a QR code, you must have a smartphone or tablet with a camera. We recommend that you download a QR code reader app that is made specifically for your phone or tablet brand.

difficult than another with the same quantitative score. It is simply insufficient to use readability data (sentence length, use of rare words, and such) and assume that this is the only information needed for gauging text complexity. Furthermore, you can't derive much guidance in terms of your teaching points from quantitative analysis alone. The art of making meaningful qualitative evaluations is best left to the judgment of a knowledgeable educator who is deeply familiar with the texts in question.

For students to access complex text, their reading experiences must include a thoughtful progression of texts, scaffolds, and instructional arrangements.

Yet teachers should be able to use the quantitative tools that are available to create a list of potential texts that they might want to use. We are not suggesting that teachers only use texts that fit within the quantitative band for their grade level, but we are concerned that there are students who are never taught to read with texts that are of an appropriate grade-level challenge. Figure 1.1 provides current readability information for a range of tools.

Qualitative Evaluation

Qualitative evaluation requires considering a text across several dimensions, including level of meaning, the use of literal versus figurative language, the clarity of the author's purpose or central idea, the overall organization, the use of graphics and visual information, and the demands of the vocabulary (see Figure 1.2 for the rubric included in the Florida B.E.S.T. Standards). Note that these descriptors mirror the teaching points

Figure 1.1 Quantitative Measures of Text Complexity		
Grade Level	Flesch-Kincaid	Lexile
K–1st	–1.3–2.18	BR–430L
2nd–3rd	1.98–5.34	420L–820L
4th–5th	4.51–7.73	740L–1010L
6th–8th	6.51–10.34	925L–1185L
9th–10th	8.32–12.12	1050L–1335L
11th–12th	10.34–14.2	1185L–1385L

Figure 1.2 Qualitative Factors of Text Complexity

Low Complexity	Mid Complexity	High Complexity
The text has a single layer of meaning explicitly stated.	Blend of explicit and implicit details; few uses of multiple meanings; isolated instances of metaphor.	The text has multiple levels of meaning and there may be intentional ambiguity.
The language of the text is literal, although there may be some rhetorical devices.	Figurative language is used to build on what has already been stated plainly in the text.	Figurative language is used throughout the text; multiple interpretations may be possible.
The author's purpose or central idea of the text is immediately obvious and clear.	The author's purpose may not be explicitly stated but is readily inferred from a reading of the text.	The author's purpose is obscure and subject to interpretation.
The text is organized in a straightforward manner with explicit transitions to guide the reader.	The text is largely organized in a straightforward manner, but may contain isolated incidences of shifts in time/place, focus, or pacing.	The text is organized in a way that initially obscures meaning and has the reader build to an understanding.
Graphics are simple and restate what is written in the text.	Graphics are not essential to understanding the text but do expand on the information found in the text.	Graphics are essential to the understanding of the text and contain information not expressed in the written text.
Vocabulary consists primarily of commonly used words. These words are used literally, not figuratively.	The text uses some domain-specific words, academic vocabulary, archaic terms, or terms that can read with ambiguity.	The text frequently uses domain-specific words, academic vocabulary, archaic terms, or terms that can read with ambiguity.

Source: Florida Department of Education (2020, p. 149).

we rely on during instruction. A given text is going to be variously more or less difficult within each of these areas, and it is unlikely that any text would be uniformly difficult across all four. *Give Bees a Chance* by Bethany Barton is a fairly straightforward text that explains the contributions of bees in our world. On the other hand, *Night* (Wiesel, 1982) uses a difficult structure—flashback—that can confuse readers.

Student-Centered Considerations

Quantitative and qualitative dimensions are solely about the characteristics of the text itself. The third facet in determining text complexity, however, takes into account the student. This last facet is where teaching lies and in fact is the central theme of this book. We will return to this throughout these chapters, but for now, we want to consider the reader. There are myriad books to select from (see Figure 1.3 for a rubric for this aspect), but only a few will make their way to your classroom or school. This aspect of text complexity ensures that teachers consider their students, the students sitting in front of them, when they select reading materials. That does not mean that students are limited to texts that they can already read, but it does mean that teachers have discretion in selecting texts that they believe will help their students grow as readers. As we will explore throughout this book, there are times when students read less complex texts and times when they read more complex texts. In reality, text complexity is a balancing act between providing sufficient opportunities for students to struggle and enough practice for them to develop habits. Teachers should consider the following when they select texts for students to read:

When it comes to reading challenging texts, students must be adequately supported to unlock the meanings hidden within.

- provide students with examples of quality writing that mentor them as writers themselves;
- grant students access to excellent illustrations;
- allow students to see themselves—their religion, ethnicity, language, and culture—in the selected texts;
- permit students to interact—through the act of reading— with people who have different experiences and beliefs;
- depict a variety of family structures;
- offer a balanced portrayal of gender identities and roles in terms of the depiction of the characters and what the characters do; and
- interrupt gender, racial, or ability stereotypes.

Another way to find quality books is to review titles that have received national and international recognition. For example, the American Library Association awards the Newbery (for writing) and the Caldecott (for illustration) each year for the best children's books. The same organization presents the Coretta Scott King award to outstanding African American authors and illustrators of books for children and young adults. The University of Texas offers the Tomás Rivera award to children's books that depict the Mexican American experience. The Orbus Pictus award is given by the National Council of Teachers of English for outstanding nonfiction written for children. The Hans Christian Andersen medal is presented biennially by the International Board of Books for

Figure 1.3 Student-Centered Considerations

Student-Centered		
Low Complexity	Mid Complexity	High Complexity
Students can fully understand the text without specific background knowledge.	Students with limited background knowledge may understand the text, but some levels of meaning may be impeded by lack of prior exposure.	For students to fully understand the text, they must have background knowledge of the topic.
The text is understood by the student without the student consciously applying comprehension strategies.	The text is such that the student can read without fatigue and can apply comprehension strategies to understand the text.	The text may demand stamina, comprehension, and inferential skills at the upper boundary of the student's developmental level.
The themes and details in the text are well within the student's developmental level of understanding and appropriate to the student's age level.	The themes and details in the text are within the student's developmental level of understanding, and while some subject matter may be sensitive, it is appropriate to the student's age level.	The themes and details in the text are at the upper boundary of the student's developmental level of understanding. Some subject matter may be sensitive but is appropriate to the student's age level.
The task associated with the text is of a low content complexity level, involving one cognitive step.	The task associated with the text is of mid-level complexity, involving multiple cognitive steps, some of which are at the recall level.	The task associated with the text is of a high content complexity level, involving multiple cognitive steps.

Source: Florida Department of Education (2020, p. 150).

Young People in recognition of the body of work of an author and of an illustrator. Each state awards a series of young reader medals for books that are particularly popular with students in the state. The state reading association or library association will have a list of these awards by year. In addition, the International Reading Association created the Children's Choice, Teen Choice, and Teachers' Choices awards.

Understanding the quantitative and qualitative properties of texts is essential, as are the considerations regarding the reader. While these are helpful categories, they do not provide instructional guidance for teachers hoping to build their students' comprehension of the texts. What do we do with complex texts once we have them? It's important to remember that there is no evidence that students can independently learn from books they can't read (Allington, 2002). When it comes to reading challenging texts, students must be adequately supported to unlock the meanings hidden within.

▶ Reading Closely and Carefully

Selecting a text is more than simply choosing a title from a list or a bookshelf. We have developed a decision pathway to help teachers select texts for their students (see Figure 1.4). Sometimes, the text is great and might be useful. In those cases, consider path 1 and ask yourself if the text meets your instructional purpose, learning intention, or objective. Continue through the questions in path 1 to determine if the text is an appropriate choice. Other times, students need instruction in some aspect of reading. For example, if a group of fifth graders needed additional instruction to "explain the development of stated or implied theme(s) throughout a literary text," the selected text would need to provide that opportunity and the teacher would follow path 2. Finally, students may need to build their knowledge base, especially if they are going to be able to read more widely about a topic. In that case, the teacher would select path 3 and consider the questions in that column before deciding on a specific text.

The intent of close reading is to foster critical thinking skills to deepen comprehension, a key aspect of the Florida B.E.S.T. Standards.

Much attention has been given to the process of close reading, which relies on repeated readings of short passages of complex texts. A key purpose of close reading is to encourage students to examine in detail what the text has to say. The first assumption behind the practice of close reading is that the text is worthy; not everything we read requires this kind of inspection. However, understanding the text itself is necessary for comprehension and is key to making the kind of analytic and evaluative judgments that mark a competent reader. One question we often hear is in regard to the use of close reading practices with students who are not yet fully independent readers. It is helpful to keep in mind that the intent of close reading is to foster critical thinking skills to deepen comprehension, a key aspect of the Florida B.E.S.T. Standards. Therefore, the thinking skills needed for close reading should begin in kindergarten. Although the delivery of the lesson is somewhat different when working with emergent readers, the intention is the same. The use of close reading in primary grades will be discussed in greater detail in Chapter 3.

Video 1.2

Doug discusses close reading.
resources.corwin.com/ rigorousreadingfla

We apply the same reasoning when working with students with disabilities. It is essential that they receive access to the general curriculum, as stated in both federal law and widely accepted best practices. Our experiences have shown us that close reading is especially useful for these and other students for whom a "one and done" reading of a text is not

Figure 1.4 Decision Pathways for Selecting Texts

Path 1 It's a Fantastic Text . . .	Path 2 My Students Need Reading Instruction About . . .	Path 3 I Want to Build My Students' Knowledge About . . .
What are my learning intentions?	What are my learning intentions?	What are my learning intentions?
Text Consideration: What are the qualitative and quantitative characteristics of the proposed text?	**Reader Consideration:** What are the reader's (or readers') cognitive capabilities, motivation, knowledge, and experiences?	**Reader Consideration:** What are the reader's (or readers') cognitive capabilities, motivation, knowledge, and experiences?
Reader Consideration: What are the reader's (or readers') cognitive capabilities, motivation, knowledge, and experiences?	**Text Consideration:** What are the qualitative and quantitative characteristics of the proposed text?	**Text Consideration:** What are the qualitative and quantitative characteristics of the proposed text?
Gap Analysis: What gap exists between the reader and the text I am considering?	**Gap Analysis:** What gap exists between the reader and the text I am considering?	**Gap Analysis:** What gap exists between the reader and the text I am considering?
Task Consideration: What instructional arrangement will best address this gap (teacher-led, peer-led, or independent)?	**Task Consideration:** What instructional arrangement will best address this gap (teacher-led, peer-led, or independent)?	**Task Consideration:** What instructional arrangement will best address this gap (teacher-led, peer-led, or independent)?
Text–Task Suitability: Does the proposed text align with the proposed task?	**Text–Task Suitability:** Does the proposed text align with the proposed task?	**Text–Task Suitability:** Does the proposed text align with the proposed task?
If **yes**, finalize decision and monitor progress toward identified learning intentions. If **no**, return to task consideration.	If **yes**, finalize decision and monitor progress toward learning intentions. If **no**, return to text consideration.	If **yes**, finalize decision and monitor progress toward learning intentions. If **no**, return to text and task considerations.

Source: Fisher, Frey, and Lapp (2016).

sufficient. Close reading affords students with the gift of time to linger with a piece of text. While we have known for decades that multiple readings are essential for deep understanding, in practice, teachers have rarely afforded students with the time to do so. Some of the greatest gains we have witnessed in our own classrooms have been with students who have otherwise struggled as readers.

Reading comprehension is not a skill that exists in a vacuum between the reader and the text immediately in front of her; it also hinges on the accumulation of texts and experiences that she has been exposed to.

There has been debate about the role of activating prior knowledge in a close reading. Reading comprehension is not a skill that exists in a vacuum between the reader and the text immediately in front of her; it also hinges on the accumulation of the many texts and experiences that she has been exposed to throughout her lifetime (e.g., Rosenblatt, 2003). Therefore, a competent reader links her prior knowledge to the new information she is experiencing. We believe that thoughtful reading teachers must encourage students to analyze, make judgments, synthesize across multiple sources of information, formulate opinions, and create new products. To do this, they should be integrating what they have learned from the text with their prior knowledge and experiences. But we share the concern that, in too many cases, the rush to engage students in these critical thinking skills has meant that relatively little time is allocated for eyes on the text. Instead, after extensive pre-teaching of the content of the text by the teacher, the text is all too often given a quick once over. In these cases, true integration doesn't take place; instead, students are mostly drawing on what they already know. It's hard to make forward progress when you're mostly just treading water.

If students are going to access complex texts, they must been given the time to read and reread, to respond to questions that encourage them to return to the text, and to discuss their ideas in the company of others. A strong textual foundation also makes it possible for them to engage in critical thinking skills. It's analogous to a ladder: It doesn't matter how tall the ladder is if the lower rungs are not solid. In our own classrooms, we are witnessing what is happening with our students who struggle to read. We are finding that spending more time on the textual foundations—the lower rungs of the ladder—is making it possible for them to analyze, evaluate, and create.

Developing readers must apprentice to the kinds of problem-solving strategies that expert readers use when their comprehension breaks down. In part, this occurs when their teachers model, as we will discuss in the next chapter. But students also need to practice what they have been taught. When it comes to using complex text, teachers should expect comprehension to break down regularly, and they should seize the opportunities these breakdowns present. These are ideal for showing students how problem-solving comprehension strategies are summoned so that, over time, they become a part of their repertoire as skilled readers (Afflerbach, Pearson, & Paris, 2008). Simply said, this is how students will develop the reading and thinking skills required in the

Florida B.E.S.T. Standards. Consider, as an example, the grade 3 expectation that students "explain a theme and how it develops, using details, in a literary text" (Florida Department of Education, 2020, p. 13). If the texts lack complexity, the key ideas and details will be obvious and students will not make errors; thus, no learning can occur. By using complex texts, in this case a text that has key ideas that are less obvious, students can learn to notice the details that eventually allow them to uncover the information. Will they get it right the first time? Probably not. They need intentional instruction, including the access points that we describe in this book.

▶ Accessing Complex Texts Through a Gradual Release of Responsibility

For students to access complex texts, they need intentional instruction that provides them with *access* to deep comprehension. In this book, we've identified five "access points," that is, five ways to intentionally guide students' comprehension of complex text. The framework that allows for the implementation of this type of intentional instruction is known as *gradual release of responsibility* (e.g., Fisher & Frey, 2008; Pearson & Fielding, 1991).

Our interpretation of the gradual release of responsibility model includes the following five phases. Importantly, these are not presented in a prescriptive order. Rather, they can be combined, and teachers can start anywhere. For example, a group of students might enter the classroom and be asked to complete a journal entry about the text the class is reading (independent) and then be invited to share their thinking with a peer (collaborative) while the teacher listens in to identify gaps in understanding so that she can model her thinking and then set the learning intention for the day. She could also identify gaps in understanding for her guided instruction and following her modeling, students may be asked to work independently or collaboratively again. The five components we look for in a lesson designed around the gradual release of responsibility framework include:

- *Learning intentions*: Teachers identify daily learning intentions based on grade-level standards and communicate the expected learning outcomes to students. Also, given the number of English language learners and standard English learners, teachers analyze the content to determine to students as well. Further, teachers identify the social aspects of learning

Video 1.3

Doug talks about the gradual release of responsibility. *resources.corwin.com/ rigorousreadingfla*

For students to access complex texts, they need intentional instruction that provides them with access to deep comprehension.

and communicate those expectations to students. The evidence for this component was summarized by Marzano, Pickering, and Pollock (2002).

- *Modeling*: Students are provided an example of the thinking required to complete each task. The teacher, not other students, shares his or her thinking while reading such that students get a glimpse inside the mind of an expert. As Duffy (2014) pointed out, "The only way to model thinking is to talk about how to do it. That is, we provide a verbal description of the thinking one does or, more accurately, an *approximation* of the thinking involved" (p. 11).

- *Guided instruction*: Through the strategic use of prompts, cues, and questions, teachers transfer some of the responsibility for learning to students. Typically, this occurs in needs-based groups of three to six students who have been purposefully selected based on formative assessment data (Avalos, Plasencia, Chavez, & Rascón, 2007/2008). Guided instruction can also occur with the whole class or with individual students as teachers address errors without telling students the answers.

- *Collaborative learning*: Students complete collaborative learning activities designed to provide them opportunities to use language and explore the content. The tasks must be structured to build on students' knowledge and be differentiated so as to not cause stress for students who currently perform below grade level (Matthews & Kesner, 2003). As we will see in the chapter on collaborative learning, some tasks include individual accountability as part of the group interaction (Johnson, Johnson, & Holubec, 2008), which allows teachers to check for understanding.

- *Independent learning*: As part of the gradual release of responsibility, students must apply what they have learned, especially in new situations or contexts (Harvey & Chickie-Wolf, 2007). Although independent learning is the goal of education, students are often assigned independent tasks for which they do not yet have the skills to complete alone. Some tasks, such as independent reading, writing prompts, and journaling, can occur in the classroom. Others, especially spiral review tasks, can be completed outside of the school day, either in an after-school program or at home.

▶ The Organization of Learning Expectations in Florida

As you may have noticed, we have quoted several Florida B.E.S.T. Standards in this chapter. Before we conclude this chapter, a brief overview of the organizational structure of these standards is warranted. Florida B.E.S.T. Standards feature four strands (p. 8): Foundations, Reading, Communication, and Vocabulary. But these strands are further divided into standards as follows:

- **Foundations:** This strand is divided into two standards: learning and applying foundational reading skills and applying foundational reading skills for secondary students needing reading interventions.
- **Reading:** This strand is divided into three standards: reading prose and poetry, reading informational text, and reading across genres.
- **Communication:** This strand is divided into five standards: communicating through writing, communicating orally, following conventions, researching, and creating and collaborating.
- **Vocabulary:** This strand has one standard: finding meaning.

Some of the standards contain clarifications. These are designed to help educators understand the language of the standard and to add details that are not included in the standards. For example, in second grade, in the area of reading informational texts, students are expected to "compare and contrast important details presented by two texts on the same topic or theme." This standard contains two clarifications:

> *Clarification 1:* For literary texts, students can compare and contrast story elements such as characters, illustrations, and sequence of events.

Clarification 2: The different versions may be of the same or different formats.

Importantly, the standards (other than foundations) are designed for increased vertical alignment. In a given grade level, some of the words in a standard are bold, meaning that those ideas were not included in previous grade levels and thus should be the focus of instruction for students at that level. For example, the standard related to Perspective and Point of View can be analyzed vertically:

R.1.3 Perspective and Point of View	
ELA.12.R.1.3	**Evaluate the development** of character perspective, **including** conflicting perspectives.
ELA.11.R.1.3	Analyze **the author's choices in using juxtaposition to define** character perspective.
ELA.10.R.1.3	Analyze **coming of age experiences reflected in a text and how the author represents conflicting perspectives.**
ELA.9.R.1.3	Analyze **the influence of narrator perspective on a text, explaining how the author creates irony or satire.**
ELA.8.R.1.3	**Analyze how an author develops and individualizes the perspectives of different characters.**
ELA.7.R.1.3	Explain the influence of narrator(s), **including unreliable narrator(s)**, and/or shifts in point of view in a literary text.
ELA.6.R.1.3	**Explain the influence of multiple narrators and/or shifts in point of view in a literary text.**
ELA.5.R.1.3	**Describe how an author develops** a character's perspective in a literary text.
ELA.4.R.1.3	Identify **the narrator's point of view and explain the difference between a narrator's point of view and character perspective** in a literary text.
ELA.3.R.1.3	**Explain** different characters' perspectives in a literary text.
ELA.2.R.1.3	Identify **different characters' perspectives in a literary text.**
ELA.1.R.1.3	Explain **who is telling the story using context clues.**
ELA.K.R.1.3	**Explain the roles of author and illustrator of a story.**

Source: Florida Department of Education (2020, p. 14).

There are other standards that repeat the same expectation across several grades. For example, the standard on finding meaning, part of the vocabulary stand, for students in Grades K, 1, 2, 3, 4, and 5 reads: "Use grade-level academic vocabulary appropriately in speaking and writing."

Similarly, Grades 6, 7, 8, 9, 10, 11, and 12 all have the same standard related to paraphrasing and summarizing: "Paraphrase content from grade-level texts."

Both of these standards, and several others, highlight the fact that access to complex texts is critical if students are to succeed in Florida. The remainder of this book focuses on the access points teachers can use to ensure that students do, in fact, access complex texts.

▶ Organization of *Rigorous Reading, Florida Edition*

In the remainder of this book, we describe in detail each access point, always through the lens of complex texts. The chapters are as follows:

- Chapter 2, "Access Point One: Modeling and Learning Intentions," describes the first access point—establishing the expectations or objectives of the lesson—and explains the ways that teachers can model their critical thinking for students as they read. In this chapter, we discuss the use of think-alouds and interactive shared readings, with special attention on the modeling of annotation skills.
- Chapter 3, "Access Point Two: Close and Scaffolded Reading Instruction," describes the second access point. The practice of close reading, which emphasizes repeated readings, discussion, and critical thinking, requires scaffolded instruction. Text-dependent questions, prompts, and cues form the basis of these scaffolds and provide students with the teacher-supported experiences they need to read increasingly complex texts.

Although independent learning is the goal of education, students are often assigned independent tasks for which they do not yet have the skills to complete alone.

The intention behind effective instruction is for students to expand their capacity to deeply understand these kinds of complex texts outside the company of their teachers. It is this understanding that lies at the heart of college and career readiness.

- Chapter 4, "Access Point Three: Collaborative Conversations," describes the third access point. These peer-led learning experiences require tasks that encourage students to interact and to apply what they have learned through close reading to develop deeper understandings of complex texts. In this chapter, we discuss a number of ways that teachers can facilitate student-to-student interactions, including literature circles, discussion roundtables, reciprocal teaching, and collaborative strategic reading.

- Chapter 5, "Access Point Four: An Independent Reading Staircase," focuses on students' ability to climb the figurative reading staircase as they apply what they have learned and read increasingly complex texts independently. While they may be reading individually, they are not reading alone, and well-designed instruction is essential in this phase. This chapter explains how to craft this instruction through the use of texts that build background knowledge and through peer-conferencing strategies that foster metacognitive awareness.

- Chapter 6, "Access Point Five: Assessing Students' Understanding," concerns itself with demonstrating understanding and assessing performance. These practices are not only for the teacher to use when measuring mastery but also for students to use to propel future learning. This chapter focuses on what occurs after reading, including feedback and assessment.

Doug's and Nancy's teachers that you met in the opening of this chapter, however well meaning, didn't know how to use these access points. Doug's teacher released cognitive responsibility much too suddenly, and he was left to try to find an outside source of information because he didn't know how to locate it within the text. Nancy's teacher never released any of the responsibility and did too much of the cognitive heavy lifting for her students. The teacher's assessments focused on the wrong measures, and she never did figure out that Nancy hadn't read the book. In using a range of access points, teachers can avoid these all-too-common pitfalls and balance support with challenge.

▶ Summary

One method for measuring text complexity is quantitative and relies on the number and types of words in the text; this measure is useful for situating a text within a grade band. However, this method of measurement does not uncover the qualitative values that render a text more or less complex. Analyzing a text qualitatively gives us insight into *what* to teach. The third facet of complexity concerns the reader, which informs *how* we teach complex texts. As students read these texts closely, they need support and instruction on how to identify textual elements and mine texts for understanding, as well as on how to use comprehension strategies to repair meaning when it becomes muddled. The intention behind effective instruction is for students to expand their capacity to deeply understand these kinds of complex texts outside the company of their teachers. It is this understanding that lies at the heart of college and career readiness. By equipping students to take on an ever-widening range of texts, we afford them their independence and extend their understanding of and influence on the biological, social, and physical world around them.

iStock.com/JohnnGreig

Access Point One

Modeling and Learning Intentions

M s. Carver asks her students to get out their copies of *Number the Stars* (Lowry, 1989) while she places her copy of the book on the document camera. "Scholars," she begins,

> Today we're going to notice the specific words that the
> author has chosen and practice asking questions while
> we read. I'm going to share some of my thinking with
> you, especially about the author's words and the questions
> I have when I am reading. I'll give you a chance to try it
> with your reading partner.

After leading a discussion of the plot thus far, she begins to read while students follow silently in their books (her thinking aloud is italicized).

"Your names?" the officer barked.

"Annemarie Johansen. And this is my sister—"

"Quiet! Let her speak for herself. Your name?" He was glaring at Ellen. *"Barked" and "glaring" are words the author is using to help me imagine this Nazi officer's anger. The author's word choice is important and in this case helps me think about the seriousness of the situation.*

Ellen swallowed. "Lise," she said, and cleared her throat. "Lise Johansen." *I know why she's lying. She doesn't want them to know she's Jewish so she pretends to be a member of the family. I'll bet the Johansens will also lie for Ellen.*

The officer stared at them grimly. "Now," Mama said in a strong voice, "you have seen that we are not hiding anything. May my children go back to bed?" *I was right. That's just what Mrs. Johansen did.*

The officer ignored her. Suddenly he grabbed a handful of Ellen's hair. Ellen winced. *Why would he pull Ellen's hair? Does he suspect something?*

He laughed scornfully. "You have a blond child sleeping in the other room. And you have this blond daughter—" he gestured toward Annemarie with his head. "Where did you get the dark-haired one?" *Oh, no! What will the Johansens say? Now I understand why the title of this chapter is "Who Is the Dark-Haired One?"* (Lowry, 1989, pp. 46–47).

Video 2.1

Teacher models comprehension strategies.
resources.corwin.com/ rigorousreadingfla

After discussing the content of the passage, Ms. Carver leads a discussion about the think-aloud. "What are the ways I helped myself to understand what was happening in the text?" she asks. Jerome offers, "You made predictions about what would happen next." Delia adds, "You asked questions, like when the Nazi pulled Ellen's hair." While students respond, Ms. Carver records their ideas on chart paper. When finished, the list reads,

- Analyze word choices
- Make predictions and confirmations
- Ask questions
- Make connections to the title
- Visualize
- Think about what we already know about a character

She asks students to listen to the next portion of the text and make suggestions about predictive statements and questions. She pauses after every few sentences to prompt suggestions and writes their ideas on a second piece of chart paper. They continue to practice as a class using the next few pages of text. After several cycles of modeling and scaffolding, she asks students to work in pairs; each student will read a page from the book to the other while using think-aloud statements to support their comprehension.

Accessing complex texts requires structured time for students to work through new strategies and practice skills. Of course, students should know what they are expected to learn. A number of studies have found that when the teacher states objectives and provides feedback, student learning increases (Hattie & Donoghue, 2016). However, while establishing purpose through learning intentions primes learning, it does not ensure that it will occur; priming is insufficient without further instruction. Simply telling students what they are to learn doesn't guarantee they will learn it. A second technique for helping students learn new concepts and skills includes modeling through demonstration, that is, stopping to emphasize the parts of a text that offer examples of the stated learning intentions. A planning template appears in Figure 2.1.

> *A number of studies have found that when the teacher states objectives and provides feedback, student learning increases.*

There are a wide range of topics for which teachers can provide models. This book centers on the topic of complex texts. It is important to note that Ms. Carver did not select a text that her students could read independently or even one that they could read with a little assistance. She selected a complex text that required intentional instruction. As noted in the discussion about the lesson, there are places in a given complex text that require teacher modeling or thinking aloud. Other parts of the text might be approproriate for close readings, collaborative conversations, partner reading, or independent reading. Teachers must identify the appropriate task for the text. To ensure that students can access complex texts, their teachers must first select complex texts and then model their thinking about the text. This type of teaching requires active involvement and shared responsibility between teachers and their students.

▶ Accessing Complex Text Requires Modeling

As Wilhelm (2001) notes, "[T]eachers model their thinking by voicing all the things they are noticing, doing, seeing, feeling, and asking as they process the text" (p. 26). In other words, the idea is that the teacher explicitly

Figure 2.1   Planning Learning Intentions and Modeling

Assessed Need: I have noticed that the students in my classroom need to work on:

Standards:

Text I will use:

Materials needed for this lesson are:

Learning intentions for the lesson are:

Model

• Parts to emphasize

Figure 2.1 (Continued)

Scaffold

- Questions to ask

Assess

- These are the students who need extra support

Practice

- Students will practice using the strategy or skill during

Reflection

- What did I notice about what my students understood?

- What did I notice about my students' misunderstandings?

or intentionally models the strategies that readers can use as they read. Over time and with practice, students will develop habits based on the strategies that their teachers model. They will no longer need to stop reading to visualize or predict; rather, these behaviors will occur automatically. But as knowledge and skills are obtained, students may need to be reintroduced to comprehension strategies and their application to more complex texts. All readers regularly fall back on strategies for resolving confusions when meaning breaks down. Once comprehension is regained, the reader continues. An important aspect of reading instruction is that teachers show students how and when to use these strategies when they get stuck. That's precisely why we don't want to excuse students who struggle to read from this kind of instruction. Arguably, they are the ones who can benefit the most from it. Because it is the teacher who is assuming most of the cognitive load during modeling, all students can access the text. To distance struggling students from this instruction is to magnify the difficulties they already possess. In other words, how would you learn to repair something if you were systematically excused every time someone began using a tool?

Video 2.2

Teacher models for her students.
resources.corwin.com/ rigorousreadingfla

Teachers can model any number of things that they want their students to learn, from how to interact with peers to how to compose an essay. In this book, we're addressing the topic of accessing complex text, so we will focus our discussion of modeling around the factors that contribute to text complexity. At the beginning of this chapter, Ms. Carver focused on vocabulary and explicit and implicit details as she modeled from *Number the Stars*. She knew these elements would factor into her students' comprehension of the text, and she used a think-aloud process to give voice to the ways she maintained her understanding of the passage.

We want students to recognize that complex texts require more from us as readers than those readings that are a more comfortable fit. Novice readers make the mistake of approaching all texts as equivalent, when they are not. In too many cases, when the text is challenging, they turn away and give up. As an expert reader, you activate different processes depending on the level of complexity you encounter. You know that you'll need to make notes for yourself when you're reading a James Joyce novel with your book club. You know how to look up an unfamiliar tax code in the manual that accompanied your annual tax return forms. When you encounter an unknown term while reading about the side effects listed in your prescription medicine insert, you consult several trusted resources. Novice readers don't automatically do these things.

Modeling is a time when you highlight the areas that you predict will be difficult for students, and you show them how you resolve comprehension problems. In addition, it is an important opportunity to show them how you interact with complex text.

Below, we will discuss three aspects of modeling and two methods for doing so:

- Model that which is difficult for students
- Model ways to resolve problems
- Model how you interact with text
- Model through think-alouds
- Model through interactive shared readings

Taken together, what you are really modeling are the habits of active readers when confronted with challenging text. You are modeling persistence and a willingness to stick with something more difficult because it's worth it.

Model That Which Is Difficult for Students

The first principle of modeling is that you are selective in what you model. There's not much point in modeling what students already know how to do, and in any case, it is not going to provide them with access to a complex text. Instead, analyze the text in advance for the elements of text complexity (see Figure 1.2) and choose one or two aspects to highlight through your modeling.

When Mr. Jefferson's first-grade class was reading *The Three Little Wolves and the Big Bad Pig* (Trivizas, 1993), he knew that his students would not have difficulty with prior knowledge as they had been comparing and contrasting for several weeks. He also knew that his students would not have trouble understanding "texts on the same topic." However, the vocabulary demand was higher, with individual words such as *croquet*, *sledgehammer*, *concrete*, and *battledore and shuttlecock* likely to cause his students some confusion. In addition, he knew that he would have to model his thinking about the "who is telling the story using context clues" and the importance of the illustrations in conveying meaning.

At one point while modeling the text, Mr. Jefferson said,

> I want to reread this part because I think I'm getting
> confused. I think that the traditional story is getting in the
> way. The pig is the bad guy in this story because he's the one
> huffing and puffing and trying to blow the house down.

Novice readers make the mistake of approaching all texts as equivalent, when they are not. In too many cases, when the text is challenging, they turn away and give up.

Later in the text, Mr. Jefferson said,

> I'm not sure that I've ever heard the phrase *battledore and shuttlecock* before. When I look at the picture, I see the wolves playing a game that looks like tennis, but there isn't a ball. It reminds me of badminton. It's a strange little thing that they're hitting back and forth. That must be the game that they're playing because the author says that they are playing *battledore and shuttlecock* in the garden when they see the big bad pig.

Notice that Mr. Jefferson focuses his modeling on expectations from the standards that he knows his students have not yet mastered. Knowing the expectations and students' current levels of performance allows teachers to teach in the gap between the known and unknown.

One interesting aspect of the Florida standards are the "expectations" or overarching skills that run through every component of language arts. These expectations include the following:

- Cite evidence to explain and justify reasoning.
- Read and comprehend grade-level complex texts proficiently.
- Make inferences to support comprehension.
- Use appropriate collaborative techniques and active listening skills when engaging in discussions in a variety of situations.
- Use the accepted rules governing a specific format to create quality work.
- Use appropriate voice and tone when speaking or writing. (Florida Department of Education, 2020, p. 147)

For students to accomplish these things, their teachers need to regularly model using appropriately complex texts. These expectations will not develop in a single lesson or even a unit. They are going to take time. Take inferencing, for example. Students need to be taught what the term means, and they need to see their teachers inference often. Inferencing is much more difficult than "reading between the lines" and is highly influenced by the implications of the author. It's going to take a lot of teacher modeling across a range of texts for students to develop the habit of making inferences, not to mention the other expectations listed in the standards.

Model Ways to Resolve Problems

The second principle of modeling is that you model ways to resolve problems and confusions. Complex text by definition is going to challenge students' understanding. Modeling is an ideal time to show students how you get yourself going again when comprehension breaks down. Often, it is the vocabulary that interferes with understanding. It is impossible to try to directly teach all of the words students will encounter as they read. Instead, teachers must help students build habits related to word solving. As the Florida standards note, students in Grades 4, 5, 6, 7, 8, 9, 10, 11, and 12 must learn to "use context clues, figurative language, word relationships, reference materials, and/or background knowledge to determine the meaning of multiple-meaning and unknown words and phrases, appropriate to grade level" (Florida Department of Education, 2020, p. 25). In addition, there is an entire standard on morphology that requires students to understand word parts, such as roots, bases, and affixes.

Structural Analysis: Looking Inside Words

When readers come to an unknown word, one of the things that they can do is look inside the word to see if there are any clues to the word's meaning. Understanding morphology, including prefixes, suffixes, roots, bases, and cognates, helps the reader make an educated guess about an unknown word. For example, if the reader has never been exposed to the word *paleozoology*, she or he can make an educated guess about this field using knowledge about prefixes and suffixes. In fact, the word is fairly easy to figure out when you remember that *paleo* means old or ancient, *zoo* relates to animals, and *-ology* relates to the study of something.

But simply providing students with a morphology list is not likely to change their behavior when they come to unknown words. Instead, teachers need to model the use of morphology in understanding words. For example, while reading a sentence that contained the word *heterozygous*, the biology teacher modeled his use of morphology saying, "I know that *hetero* means different, so this must be the one that has two different alleles, or different versions, of a specific gene."

Of course, morphology does not always work, and students should be provided with examples that remind them to check other clues as well. Our favorite example of this occurred in an English as a Second Language classroom when the teacher got to the word *repeat*. She said,

Modeling is an ideal time to show students how you get yourself going again when comprehension breaks down. Teachers must help students build habits related to word solving.

Video 2.3

Elementary teacher models word solving.
resources.corwin.com/ rigorousreadingfla

Video 2.4

High school
teacher models
word solving.
*resources.corwin.com/
rigorousreadingfla*

I got this one. I know that *re-* means to do again. So I'm going to *peat* again. Wait, I have no idea what that means! I better check the context clues and look outside the word to see if I can figure this out.

Context Clues: Looking Outside Words

In addition to looking inside words, students have to be taught to look outside of words to figure out their meaning. This happens through an understanding of context clues. Although context clues are not infallible, they can be helpful. There are a number of different kinds of context clues, such as embedded synonyms, antonyms, direct definitions, and the use of punctuation. Again, students need to be taught how to use these tools. Modeling provides students with examples that can be built into habits.

For example, when reading about the "supermoon" predicted for January 2, 2018, the teacher noted the word *fatalities* in the news report. There had been quite a bit of news coverage around the world that this astronomical event, which brought the Moon into close range of the Earth, would cause widespread flooding and earthquakes. She made the connection between *fatalities* in the beginning of the sentence and the use of "the number dead" later in the sentence. Another example occurred when the teacher modeled using punctuation, in this case a dependent clause that contained additional and specific information about a more difficult word. Just as we discussed with word parts, teachers should model when the use of context clues fails.

Again, the goal is for students to develop a habit that they can use independently when they come across unknown words. Like most of the systems we use when reading and trying to make meaning, they don't always work. When these two systems—word parts and context clues—fail, it's time to look further outside the word and use resources.

Using Resources: Looking Further Outside Words

"When all else fails, look it up" is a common motto of teachers, and for good reason. When the systems we have for figuring out unknown words within a text do not help, it's time to turn our attention to the resources we have at our disposal. Once upon a time, that was limited to printed dictionaries and glossaries. Today, we have a plethora of resources at our fingertips because of the Internet. For example, the visual dictionary (http://visual.merriam-webster.com) is a great resource that students can be taught to use. The same holds for the many specialized dictionaries, such as the following:

> *In addition to looking inside words, students have to be taught to look outside of words to figure out their meaning. This happens through an understanding of context clues.*

- **Science:** http://www.thesciencedictionary.com
- **History:** http://www.babylon.com/define/52/History-Dictionary.html
- **Mathematics:** http://www.amathsdictionaryforkids.com
- **Art:** http://www.artlex.com
- **Sports and fitness**: http://dictionary.babylon.com/sports

As with word parts and context clues, teachers should model their use of resources such as these and model the appropriate ways to ask other people for help. This can be as simple as calling a friend on the classroom phone or texting someone for more information.

Modeling word solving should be integrated with other approaches to understanding the text, such as those based on comprehension strategies and on using text structures and text features. We are not suggesting that teachers focus only on modeling word solving, but rather that they include word solving in their shared readings and think-alouds so that students have access to examples of expert thinking about words. It is important to emphasize that teachers should model their thinking, selecting the content of the modeling to coincide with the aspects of the text that contribute to their complexity. This is one of the keys to accessing complex texts. Modeling is not random, "whatever comes to mind," but rather purposeful instruction focused on specific identified aspects of text complexity.

Model How You Interact With Text

A third principle of modeling provides students with examples of how proficient readers act on text to support their comprehension. Complex text requires interaction with the text, yet many students approach texts rather passively. They don't know that they should be making notes to themselves, especially to guide their rereading. Annotation of text, the practice of making notes for oneself during reading, is an essential practice for closely reading complex text. As well, it is useful when writing about the text, as students consult their annotations to formulate arguments, analyze information, and make connections within and outside of the text. Importantly, these annotations have a life beyond their initial construction. They are used in discussions, and some teachers even collect the annotated texts for the purpose of assessment. Adler and Van Doren (1972) describe the most common annotation marks:

- **Underlining** for major points.
- **Vertical lines in the margin** to denote longer statements that are too long to be underlined.

Annotation methods are ideal for use during modeling, as they allow teachers to demonstrate the habits of an active reader.

- **Star, asterisk, or other doodad in the margin** to be used sparingly to emphasize the ten or dozen most important statements. You may want to fold a corner of each page where you make such a mark or place a slip of paper between the pages.
  - **Numbers in the margin** to indicate a sequence of points made by the author in development of an argument.
- **Numbers of other pages in the margin** to indicate where else in the book the author makes the same points.
- **Circling of key words or phrases** to serve much the same function as underlining.
- **Writing in the margin, or at the top or bottom of the page** to record questions (and perhaps answers) that a passage raises in your mind. (pp. 49–50)

These annotation methods are ideal for use during modeling, as they allow teachers to demonstrate the habits of an active reader. The types of annotations should be consistent with the developmental needs of students. For example, in the primary grades annotations might be confined to underlining key points and circling unfamiliar words. As students progress into the intermediate grades, teachers begin to add other marks to indicate surprise or highlight questions we may have. In our modeling of annotations, we make sure that we are also writing our observations or queries so we can consult them later. As students move into middle and high school, we add numeration of the author's arguments and claims.

Student annotation can be limited when students can't write directly on the text. We circumvent this in several ways. Sometimes we ask students to annotate on sticky notes they affix to the page. If the passage is a shorter one, we photocopy it on large paper and ask them to write in the broad margins. Some of our colleagues have developed forms to accompany a reading, and one of our colleagues asks her students to slip the text into a clear plastic protective sleeve to develop temporary annotations.

As we noted earlier, modeling with complex texts teaches students the importance of persistence when confronted with challenge. Mere exhortations to try harder are insufficient; what is modeled should be a first step in equipping students with the tools they need to resolve comprehension problems. In the next section, we will discuss two methods for modeling with complex texts: think-alouds and shared reading.

Model Through Think-Alouds

The ninth-grade earth science class is focused on live video streamed from a news agency showing the eruption of a small volcano located near the Eyjafjallajökull glacier in Iceland. The voice of the teacher narrates what he is seeing as he watches with his class. "As I'm watching this, I'm thinking about how unique this eruption is," he says. "With most volcanoes, there are earthquakes that signal something might be happening. But these volcanoes around Iceland don't give any warning. I checked on the USGS website, and the tremors were really small." He continues, "I'm also noticing that the eruption is more like a fissure. See how it's tearing here?" he gestures. "It's awfully close to this glacier. If the fissure keeps widening, it's going to have an impact on the glacier itself." The teacher concludes, "I know this area [in Iceland] is where the Eurasian and North American tectonic plates meet, because I looked on this map. I'm guessing that there's been significant movement of those plates, and this volcanic eruption is the result."

Students deserve, at some point in every lesson, to experience the curriculum from the experts' perspective. This provides them with an opportunity to imitate the expert thinking.

Without the teacher's exposure of his thinking, his students would be left to their own devices to draw conclusions about the natural disaster they were witnessing. In a matter of two minutes, the teacher demonstrated how he used his background knowledge ("I'm thinking about how unique this eruption is"), consulted resources (the U.S. Geological Survey and a tectonic plate map), applied expert noticing ("See how it's tearing here?"), and speculated ("I'm guessing that there's been significant movement"). This teacher's use of a think-aloud procedure is a quality indicator of how expertise is shared in the classroom. Students deserve, at some point in every lesson, to experience the curriculum from the experts' perspective. This provides them with an opportunity to imitate the expert thinking, almost like an apprentice would in learning a new skill. Imitating is one of the ways humans learn, and modeling taps into this system (Fisher, Frey, & Lapp, 2008). Tips for effective think-alouds can be found in Figure 2.2.

Teachers regularly use modeling and demonstration to show students how a skill, strategy, or concept is used. While often associated more closely with performance tasks like swinging a tennis racket or playing a musical instrument, modeling is equally effective for cognitive and metacognitive tasks. Modeling includes naming the task or strategy, explaining when it is used, and applying analogies to link to new learning. The teacher then demonstrates the task or strategy, alerts learners about errors to avoid, and shows them how it is

Figure 2.2 Tips for Effective Think-Alouds

Choose a short piece of text. Think-alouds are often the most effective when they are focused and well paced. A brief think-aloud delivered using a passage of one to four paragraphs will have more impact because student interest will be maintained. As well, it will prevent the temptation to model too many strategies.

Let the text tell you what to do. Don't plan to go into a think-aloud cold, without having read the text, because your teaching points will be unfocused. Read the text several times and make notes about the comprehension strategies you are using to understand the text. These notes will provide you with ideas for the content of your think-aloud. Annotate the text so you will have something to refer to as you read.

Keep your think-alouds authentic. It can be a little disconcerting to say aloud what's going on in your head. Most teachers adopt a conversational tone that mirrors the informal language people use when they are thinking. An overly academic tone will sound contrived. It's better to say, "Hey—when I read this part about the penguins, right away I saw a penguin in my mind," rather than, "I was metacognitively aware and activated my visualizing strategy to formulate an image of a penguin as I read that paragraph."

Think like a scientist, mathematician, historian, artist, literary critic . . . Your shared reading texts are chosen because they have content value. Thinking aloud doesn't mean that everyone suddenly has to be a reading or English teacher. Make your think-alouds authentic by telling students how you process text through the lens of **your** content expertise. This elevates the think-aloud because you are showing them how your understanding of content text is influenced by what you know about the content.

Tell them what you did. Using an authentic voice doesn't mean you can't name the strategy. Tell your students what strategy you used to help you comprehend. This allows them to begin to form schemas about reading comprehension. Underline or highlight words or phrases that helped you understand and encourage students to do likewise, if possible.

Resist the urge to "over-think." The meaning of the passage should not be sacrificed for the sake of the think-aloud. Don't insert so many think-alouds into the reading that the intended message is lost. Fewer well-crafted think-alouds will have far more impact than a stream-of-consciousness rap that leaves the students bewildered by what just happened.

Source: Frey, Nancy, *Improving Adolescent Literacy: Content Area Strategies at Work*, 3rd Ed., ©2012. Reprinted by permission of Pearson Education, Inc., New York, New York.

applied to check for accuracy. Modeling is often accompanied by a think-aloud procedure (Davey, 1983) to further expose the decisions made by an expert as he or she processes information. For this reason, the think-aloud consistently contains "I" statements to invite the learner into the mind of the teacher.

This is a profound shift from what most teachers are accustomed to doing. Much of classroom instruction is in the second person and is interrogative in nature ("When you look at this eruption, what do you see?"). Teaching and quizzing become the order of the day, and students walk away from the class under the false assumption that somehow the teacher just "knows" the answer. They are not made privy to the speculative, at times hesitant, thinking of the content expert. What's lost are the natural stutter-steps made by someone who is deeply knowledgeable of the complexities of the topic.

It's understandable that many teachers struggle with this part of their instruction. The majority of instruction they have encountered has been the interrogative kind. They don't have an internalized monologue of what an effective think-aloud sounds like. Therefore, it's useful to introduce teachers to some quality indicators related to modeling and thinking aloud. We've found it particularly helpful for teachers to watch each other model and then talk about how it felt, both as the person modeling and the person observing expert thinking. Some of the indicators we look for during teacher modeling include

We've found it particularly helpful for teachers to watch each other model and then talk about how it felt, both as the person modeling and the person observing expert thinking.

- naming a strategy, skill, or task;
- stating the purpose of the strategy, skill, or task;
- using "I" statements;
- demonstrating how the strategy, skill, or task is used;
- alerting learners about errors to avoid; and
- assessing the usefulness of the strategy or skill.

Importantly, after receiving adequate time in scaffolded instructional support that includes modeling, the students should be able to complete tasks using the skill or strategy that was modeled for them. In other words, modeling provides students with examples, not a recipe, that they can follow as they complete their own work.

Model Through Interactive Shared Readings

Shared reading is an instructional procedure that uses appropriately complex text that can be viewed by both the teacher and the student at the same time (Holdaway, 1979). The responsibility for reading the text is shared because the students follow the print silently while the teacher reads aloud. During subsequent rereadings, students can read aloud as well.

For younger students in kindergarten through second grade, an oversized version of a picture book measuring approximately 24 inches or more in width is commonly used. The primary advantage of using a big book is that the large print and illustrations are visible to the students. Teachers of older students often display the shared reading text on a document camera, or many provide each child with a copy to write on. In other cases, a reading from the basal or a textbook is used. At all times, the passage chosen should be one that is complex both quantitatively and qualitatively.

The interactive nature of shared readings allows teachers to move beyond simply conveying text to elevating a lesson to focus on discourse. Students at all grade levels benefit immeasurably from discussion with peers. These lessons are not passive, and they provide students with many opportunities to develop their academic language through the use of verbal expressions of ideas. In addition, they require students to listen closely not only to the text being read but to the comments of their peers as well.

Characteristics of Interactive Shared Reading Lessons

Shared reading is recognizable in the way it is delivered by the teacher. A shared reading event is likely to be short and lively, and the text is read more than once to reinforce the skills or strategies being taught. It also helps students build the habit of rereading when the text is complex. As students become comfortable, they are encouraged to read along with the teacher. Rog (2001) describes five characteristics of shared reading:

- Uses large print
- Provides brief, engaging lessons that encourage student participation
- Suits mixed-ability groups
- Includes repeated readings to reinforce concepts
- Emphasizes skills at the letter, word, sentence, and text levels

A well-constructed interactive shared reading lesson serves as an effective method for introducing key strategies and skills through active

Video 2.5

Making learning visible through learning intentions.
resources.corwin.com/ rigorousreadingfla

teaching. Shared reading allows the teacher to instruct through modeling by demonstrating how a skill or strategy is applied to a reading. After modeling, the teacher asks questions to foster discussion and provides prompts to scaffold students' understanding as they read text that is initially new to them. Students interact with one another as well to support each other as they apply the new skill or strategy.

The act of shared reading does not create readers— it is what the teacher does inside the shared reading event that makes the difference.

Of course, it is essential to remember that the act of shared reading does not create readers—it is what the teacher does inside the shared reading event that makes the difference. Like all aspects of teaching, a successful shared reading lesson requires careful planning. Effective teachers

1. craft their lessons based on the needs of the students and their grade level standards;
2. identify instructional materials that allow students to master the learning intentions; and
3. create a sequence of instruction that includes
   - modeling through demonstration,
   - scaffolding through questions and prompts, and
   - supporting through peer interactions.

In this way, students acquire important skills and strategies needed for accurate, efficient, and meaningful reading.

Pressley et al. (1992) observed a second-grade teacher use a think-aloud process during a shared reading of *Where the Wild Things Are* (Sendak, 1963). This text is complex in that it requires students to move back and forth between a realistic setting and a dreamlike one. The teacher used both visualization and prediction strategies to focus her students' attention on her anticipation of this shift:

> "That night Max wore this wolf suit and made mischief of one kind and another . . ." Boy, I can really visualize Max. He's in this monster suit and he is chasing after his dog with a fork in his hand. I think he is really starting to act crazy. I wonder what made Max act like that . . . Hm-m-m . . . I bet he was getting a little bored and wanted to go on an adventure. I think that is my prediction.

In a seventh-grade classroom, Ms. Fleck thought aloud during a shared reading to make her understanding of the opening paragraph of *Old Yeller*

(Gibson, 1956) explicit for students. Her modeling was designed to invite students into the book. The first paragraph of the book reads,

> We called him Old Yeller. The name had a sort of double meaning. One part meant that his short hair was dingy yellow, a color we called "yeller" in those days. The other meant that when he opened his head, the sound he let out came closer to being a yell than a bark. (p. 1)

We can model all we want, and do it well, but some students will still miss the point if they don't clearly understand the purpose of the lesson.

Ms. Fleck's think-aloud demonstrated the way in which a reader activates his or her prior knowledge, summarizes information, and predicts future events in the text. She said to the class,

> I like the way the author tells us how this dog was named— he got his name from the color of his fur *and* because of the sounds he makes. I think that is a great way to pick a name for a dog. I bet both of those things—his color and his bark—will be important as we read the story. The author is probably telling us this to get us ready for really important things in the pages to come. I had a dog like that. He used to make the most awful sound when he tried to bark. We never thought to call him "yeller," but wow, what a sound he could make.

Thus far we have discussed the reasons for modeling and the methods for doing so. But modeling requires active participation from the learner as well. We can model all we want, and do it well, but some students will still miss the point if they don't clearly understand the purpose of the lesson. A learning intention alerts the learner to what they should be attending to during your modeling, and how they will use it in their own learning. In the next section, we will examine the role of establishing learning intentions in order to ensure access to complex texts.

▶ Accessing Complex Text Requires a Clear Learning Intention

Each lesson should have a purpose, goal, learning intention, or objective. Teachers have known about the importance of objectives for several decades (Hunter, 1976). A clearly articulated learning intention focuses instruction, provides students with an answer to the question "why do we have to learn this?" and allows for assessment of outcomes. It is a vital component for accessing complex texts, because it alerts students to what they should attend to as you model. In addition, it prepares them for the ways they will use the modeled information later in the lesson. Yet communicating the learning intention is a teaching behavior that is often neglected. In too many classrooms, students are left to intuit the learning intention of a lesson. Simply said, establishing the purpose of the lesson facilitates student achievement (Fisher, Frey, & Hattie, 2016).

Communicating the learning intention is a teaching behavior that is often neglected. In too many classrooms, students are left to intuit the learning intention of a lesson.

But what do good learning intentions look like? It's more than simply stating the standard to students. A quality learning intention statement provides information for students about what they will learn and how they might demonstrate that understanding. A quality learning intention statement also helps the teacher plan the lesson, as the tasks students are asked to complete should align with the expected understanding. This is an important point that is easy to overlook. The learning intention drives instruction, differentiation, and assessment. It might seem like an insignificant component of quality teaching, given that it should occupy only a fraction of the lesson, but we think it's the foundation of quality lesson planning and instructional delivery.

In our work, we use *learning intention*, rather than *goal* or *objective*, because it forces us to pay attention to what the students think. Teachers write objectives, but students have to know what the intent of the lesson is. While teachers want objectives that are measurable, students want to know what they're expected to learn and why. We ask our students, "What are you learning?" rather than "What are you doing?" because we want them to notice their learning. That's why an agenda or lesson plan alone won't do. It is a list of tasks, but it doesn't address the learning expectations or intentions.

Components of the Learning Intention

There are a number of ways to think about components of a learning intention. To be clear, learning intentions should not focus on the tasks that students will complete as part of the class session or at home. Rather, they should reflect the understandings that students will gain as a result of their engagement in the lesson components. When lessons are planned with the end in mind, learning intentions are easier to develop (Wiggins & McTighe, 2005).

Content

Part of the learning intention comes from the content standards. This is, in part, why a clearly established learning intention is critical. Planning an amazing lesson for ninth graders based on seventh-grade standards will not ensure that the students reach high levels of achievement. Having a learning intention based on content standards ensures that instruction is aligned with high expectations.

Suggesting that the learning intention is based on the content standards does not mean that the learning intention *is* the standard. Most content standards take time to master. The learning intention should focus on the learning for the day. For example, it takes weeks for students to understand the causes and impact of World War II, so several learning intentions that add up to this larger picture will be required. When standards are not analyzed for their component parts and instead are used as the learning intention, students stop paying attention to them. The standards might be posted on the wall, but they're like wallpaper to students: a decoration that really doesn't have anything to do with today's work. An appropriate content learning intention for third graders might be "I am learning about the ways authors make objects sound or act like people." This is an important part of students' eventual understanding of the Florida figurative language standard, specifically that students "identify and explain **metaphors, personification, and hyperbole** in text(s)" (Florida Department of Education, 2020, p. 17).

Having a learning intention based on content standards ensures that instruction is aligned with high expectations.

Language

A second component of the learning intention relates to the ways in which students can demonstrate their understanding of the content. This is often referred to as the *language purpose*, as humans demonstrate their understanding by reading, writing, speaking, listening, and viewing. Understanding the linguistic demands of the content is critical for this component of the learning intention, which is especially valuable for English learners who are doing double the work, learning content and language simultaneously (Fisher, Frey, & Rothenberg, 2008).

To develop the language component of the learning intention, teachers should consider the following:

- Vocabulary
- Language structure
- Language function

For some lessons, the important linguistic component might be related to the *vocabulary* of the discipline. For example, in second grade, part of the learning intention might be for students to *use the terms* time, place *or* location, *or* action *when describing the setting*.

For other lessons, students need to focus on *language structure*—grammar, syntax, or signal words. For example, students learning the art of sourcing ideas might use a sentence frame, *While _____ believed _____, others disagreed* as part of their conversations with peers.

A third way to think about the language component is by determining the *function of language* that is necessary to understand the content. In other words, do students need to justify, persuade, inform, entertain, debate, or hypothesize to understand the lesson? For example, in a discussion about a particular text, part of the purpose might be to *justify your answer with evidence from the text*.

Social

The final aspect of the learning intention is the social purpose. Given that much of the learning students do will involve others and the fact that students need to learn prosocial behaviors, we believe that teachers should be clear about the expected social interactions students should have with their peers. There is a wide range of topics that students can learn socially, from taking turns to tracking the speaker to sharing ideas with others. In addition, the social and emotional development of students should be considered as teachers plan lessons that include social learning expectations.

Sample content, language, and social purposes that comprise the learning intentions can be found in Figure 2.3.

> We believe that teachers should be clear about the expected social interactions students should have with their peers.

Figure 2.3 Sample Content, Language, and Social Learning Intentions

	Content	Language	Social
Kindergarten	Notice where words start and stop	Use the *word space* or *punctuation* to identify the place where a word ends	Take turns when reading words in the sentences
Grade 5	Summarize information from an informational text	Use sequence words (first, then, then, finally)	Track speakers as they orally synthesize information
Grade 10	Identify evidence from the text in support of your claims	Justify the appropriateness of each piece of evidence	Provide growth-producing feedback to peers about their choices

Communicate the Learning Intention

Once a learning intention has been constructed, it has to be communicated to students. There are a number of ways that teachers do this. Some post it on the board and briefly talk about the learning intention and its relevance for students at the start of the learning intention. Others begin with inquiry and then invite students to talk about why they are doing what they're doing before making the learning intention more explicit. And still others verbally discuss the learning intention and then invite students to write the learning intention in their own words as part of their note-taking tasks.

Regardless of how the learning intention is established, it's important that students know the learning intention of the lesson. It tells them what to pay attention to and what will be expected of them as they learn to access complex texts. A clearly communicated learning intention increases the relevance of the lesson for students and helps the teacher remain focused on the lesson at hand without drifting too far afield and wasting valuable instructional time. In fact, this is the most common thing that teachers who begin communicating learning intentions tell us, "It really helped me stay focused." When asked about the impact of staying focused, we regularly hear "my students learn more" and "I have more than enough time to cover the standards, and cover them well." During the course of the lesson, unanticipated student misunderstandings may be revealed, and may necessitate deviation from the original instructional plan. However, even in these cases the learning intention is valuable, as it helps the teacher and the students return once again to the intended focus of the lesson.

A clearly communicated learning intention increases the relevance of the lesson for students and helps the teacher remain focused on the lesson without wasting valuable instructional time.

▶ Summary

The first access point for students to engage with complex texts is established through modeling and setting the expectations for learning. Modeling and thinking aloud provide students with a glimpse of your cognitive and metacognitive processes as you read, understand, and interact with a text. They also alert students to the fact that as an expert reader, you know you have to activate additional resources in order to make sense of the text. For that reason, it is helpful to identify in advance the elements of a text that you believe will give your students more difficulty. After all, they really don't need you to model what they already know how to do. Make sure that students witness how you solve comprehension problems and annotate the text to support subsequent readings. These efforts are likely to be wasted if students don't know what they are watching and listening for, or if they are unclear on how they will apply it. Clear learning intentions that address the content, language, and social demands of the lesson also assist students in focusing their attention.

Access Point Two

Close and Scaffolded Reading Instruction

Middle school English teacher Armando Perez invites his students to read a short story called "Eleven" by Sandra Cisneros (1991). He points out to them that they are still exploring the inner lives of characters and considering how those lives compare to their outward lives—the ones that others can see. The students read the text independently, making notes as they go. Fernando underlines several sections in the text and circles two. Following their independent reading, Mr. Perez reads the text aloud to students, pausing to think aloud in the three places that seemed to have caused them confusion. He is able to pinpoint these particular sections of the text because he walked around the classroom observing his students as they made their annotations. He could thus target his modeling on these areas of confusion.

At one point, he pauses his read-aloud and says,

> They have a lot of years and numbers in this text, but
> this says that the sweater is maybe 1,000 years old. I'm

having a hard time believing that. I'm thinking that if it really were 1,000 years old, it would be in a museum. I'm thinking that this is an example of hyperbole that is being used to make a point.

Following his modeling, Mr. Perez asks his students to talk about a couple of questions, including "How is age like an onion, at least according to the author?" and "Why does she start crying when she has to wear the sweater?" The students talk with each other about these questions, often referring back to the text to locate specific information that they want to use in their responses.

Next, Mr. Perez asks students to talk with their team about Rachel's inner life, saying, "From what the author tells us, what can we surmise is going on inside Rachel's head when her teacher says that the sweater has to belong to someone?" The students focus on the words that the character Rachel uses to describe herself, such as "skinny," and on how the author refers to her "little voice." Jeremy says, "I don't think that Rachel has confidence because she stumbles on her answer to the teacher, and then it says that she's feeling like she is three again."

Close reading is predicated on the notion that the text is well known to the teacher and deeply understood. This can be challenging for teachers of younger students, who might be tempted to view these passages rather simply.

Mr. Perez continues inviting students to provide their arguments, with evidence, as they reread the text looking for examples. They talk with their groups often and periodically are invited to share with the whole class. After having read the text at least four times, Mr. Perez asks his students to use their annotations to describe the inner life of one of the characters in the short story. He says, "You might select Rachel, but alternatively you could select Mrs. Price or Sylvia or even Phyllis. Just remember to describe the character's inner life using evidence provided from the text." As the students get to work, Mr. Perez meets with several who have struggled with tasks like this in the past, making sure that they are starting on the right track.

There are many different ways to engage students in reading. There are instructional routines that require extensive teacher support, such as shared readings, which was described in the previous chapter, and instructional routines that require extensive peer support, such as reciprocal teaching or literature circles, which are included in the next chapter. In this chapter, we focus on an instructional routine called *close reading*, known in some circles as *analytic reading*. In addition, we will focus on scaffolded reading instruction.

Figure 3.1 Comparing Close and Scaffolded Reading Instruction

	Close Reading Instruction	Scaffolded Reading Instruction
Grouping	Large or small group; heterogeneous	Small, needs-based; homogeneous
Text Difficulty	Challenging, complex grade-level texts	Challenging but tailored to the instructional needs of the group
Teacher Supports	Text-dependent questions; annotation; repeated readings	Questions to check for understanding, prompts for cognitive or metacognitive work, cues to shift attention, and direct explanations as needed
Purpose	Expose students to content that stretches their thinking and reading skills	Advance student reading skill levels; practice comprehension strategies; uncover and address errors and misconceptions

This occurs in small groups. Both are useful in providing students access to complex texts. A comparison between close and scaffolded instruction can be found in Figure 3.1.

▶ Accessing Complex Text Requires Close Reading

Close reading is not a new instructional routine; in fact, it has existed for many decades as the practice of reading a text for a level of detail not typically sought after in everyday reading (Richards, 1929). Close readings should be done with texts that are worthy and that are complex enough to warrant repeated reading and detailed investigation. As Newkirk (2010) noted, not all texts demand this level of attention. But some texts do.

In those cases, the reader has to develop a fairly sophisticated understanding of what the author actually said. A problem, as described by advocates for close reading, is that students are often encouraged to answer questions that take them away from the reading prematurely and lead them to thinking about their own experiences. Instead, as Rosenblatt (1938/1995) recommended, there must be a transaction between the reader and the text. Readers should develop an understanding of the author's words and bring their own experiences, beliefs, and ideas to bear on the text. In her words, "The reader must remain faithful to the author's text and must be alert to the potential clues concerning character and motive" (p. 11). Rosenblatt cautioned that readers might ignore elements in a text and fail to realize that they are "imputing to the author views unjustified by the text" (p. 11).

Video 3.1

Close reading with sixth-grade English language learners.
resources.corwin.com/ rigorousreadingfla

If students already knew how to do this, we would not be spending time focused on close reading. The problem is that students do not arrive already knowing how to interrogate a text and dig down into its deeper meaning. Teachers have to teach students how to do this, in both informational and literary texts. In other words, close readings are not exclusively for English teachers; close readings should be conducted in any class or content area in which complex texts play a role, whether in science, social studies, auto mechanics, art, or physical education. Whatever the content may be, close readings of that content will always require the teacher to keep several important considerations in mind: the length of the selected text, the amount of time allocated for students to reread the text, the need to limit the frontloading of information when introducing the text, and the goal of having students annotate the text, ask text-dependent questions, and engage in text-dependent after-reading activities.

In the following section, we will describe six close reading practices that guide students' understanding of complex texts:

1. Short, worthy passages
2. Students rereading
3. Limited frontloading
4. Text-dependent questions
5. Annotation
6. After-reading tasks

Short, Worthy Passages

Because close readings can be time consuming, it is best to select shorter pieces of text for instruction. These selections, typically between three and nine paragraphs in length, allow students to practice the analytic skills required of sophisticated readers. Longer, extended texts can be used to encourage students to practice the skills that they have been taught during close readings. Close reading instruction is not limited to stand-alone short texts such as news articles, poems, or short stories. Close readings can be done with short passages from longer texts, especially when a section is especially challenging and is pivotal for understanding the larger message of the text. Of course, this requires that the teacher analyze the text for its complexity and determine which parts require close reading. Close reading is predicated on the notion that the text is well known to the teacher and deeply understood. This can be challenging for teachers of younger students, who might be tempted to view these passages rather simply and not mine them for their more complex elements.

Students do not arrive already knowing how to interrogate a text and dig down into its deeper meaning. Teachers have to teach students how to do this.

Students' Rereading

As part of a close reading, students must read and reread the selected text several times. This requires that students have expanding purposes for each repeated reading. These rereadings can be completed independently, with peers, with teacher think-alouds, or any combination thereof. As noted in the example from Mr. Perez's classroom, complex texts do not give up their meaning easily or quickly. In addition to improving fluency, repeated readings contribute to the comprehension and retention of information (Millis & King, 2001) as well as enjoyment (Faust & Glenzer, 2000). The practice of rereading carries into adult life, as noted by Smith (2000), who found that to be one of the most common strategies adults use to understand text. Of course, there are a number of ways to facilitate students' rereading of the same text. Unfortunately, most readers do not like to reread things a second or third time unless there is a specific reason for doing so. During close readings, the purpose for each reading is made clear, and often, those purposes are related to looking for evidence in response to a specific question. Importantly, rereading also reduces the need for extensive frontloading.

Limited Frontloading

When students read a piece of text only one time, the teacher has to do a lot of work to ensure their understanding. In other words, the teacher is doing the heavy lifting. When students read and reread a text multiple times and talk about the text with their peers, the teacher does not have to provide as much instructional support. The rereading, discussions, and text-dependent questions do some of this. During close readings, the

Video 3.2

Student rereads and discusses a complex text in high school English.

resources.corwin.com/ rigorousreadingfla

Video 3.3

Close reading of historical information.

resources.corwin.com/ rigorousreadingfla

teacher does not provide much in the way of pre-teaching or frontloading of content. The structure of the lesson itself is the scaffolding that was once delivered through frontloading.

As with inquiry, the goal of close reading is for students themselves to figure out what is confusing and to identify resources they can use to address their confusions. It is essential that they develop the meta-cognition needed to understand difficult texts. Close reading is in part about discovering—in this case, discovering what the author meant and how to come to terms with the ideas in the text. For example, students were introduced to George Washington's "Farewell Address" in their humanities class. Consistent with a close reading approach, students read and discussed this text several times, over several days, to fully develop their understanding of the text and what role it played, and continues to play, in history. Had their teacher provided a great deal of information in advance of this reading, students might have skipped the reading entirely and focused on what the teacher said.

Revealing the content of the reading in advance is different from stating the *learning intention*. Learning intentions focus on the reasons for reading but do not provide the students with all the information about the reading. In the first lesson, the learning intention was for students to identify Washington's reasons for leaving office after his first term as president. However, he withheld the details of the content of the passage itself. In addition, had the teacher told students what to think about the text (a common problem with extensive pre-teaching), the investigative aspect would have been lost, and students would not have developed the thinking skills that they needed when encountering complex texts on their own. Through multiple readings, students were eventually able to identify the influential nature of the document on the Federalist Party development.

Close reading does not apply solely to informational texts. Consider the difference in the amount of student learning that would likely occur in following two scenarios: first, in a situation where students are told about the author's life, his reason for writing, and the historical significance of a sonnet such as "The Long Love" by Sir Thomas Wyatt; second, in a case where students are given a chance to encounter the text and struggle with the meaning. In the former, students are often told what to think, whereas in the latter, students are guided in their discovery. In an eleventh-grade English class, as this poem was discussed, one student said to another,

The lines in this poem that stand out to me are "And in mine heart doth keep his residence," and "And therein campeth, spreading his banner." These lines stand out to me because they both are examples of how Wyatt uses love as a person, not just a feeling. Using the word "his" to refer to love as someone that is within him. It's like he's possessed with love.

Later in their discussion, the students were asked to consider the extended metaphors in the poem. They had experience analyzing the metaphors in the text, understood what they were being tasked with, and were able to apply this knowledge to the poem. Another student responded,

> The major metaphor of the poem, I feel, is consistent because Wyatt talks about love as a thing living within him, within his heart and throughout the poem that does not change. At the end he even says, "But in the field with him to live or die?" Wyatt refers to love as his master and will follow him into the field.

The goal of close reading is for students themselves to figure out what is confusing and to identify resources they can use to address their confusions. It is essential that they develop the metacognition needed to understand difficult texts.

The archaic language of the poem made this more complex, and it would have been tempting to teach students about the meaning of the poem in advance of their readings. But by allowing students to wrestle with, and ultimately discover, that the poet was writing about the all-consuming power of romantic love to turn a life upside down, these students were able to locate the poem's meaning for themselves. Grounded in the text, they are now ready to extend their thinking about connections to themes in literature and in their own experiences. Too much frontloading, in this case, might have prevented this learning. However, the students didn't come to these understandings simply through rereadings and through their teacher's practice of limited frontloading. Their teacher relied on text-dependent questions to provide students with expanding purposes for rereading, and to guide their thinking.

Text-Dependent Questions

As part of every close reading, students should discuss their responses to text-dependent questions that require them to provide evidence from

Video 3.4

Close reading and text-dependent questions in upper elementary school.

resources.corwin.com/ rigorousreadingfla

Accessing complex texts doesn't mean simply having them nearby—readers actually have to read them.

the text rather than solely from their own experiences. For example, if a English teacher asked students the personal question, "Have you ever been in love?" he would have derailed the class discussion before it even began. Most of us can imagine the chaos that would have ensued as a roomful of 17-year-olds gleefully chomped down on this question. However, a commitment to fully understanding the text will still lead students to find answers to these sorts of questions as they begin to see themselves and the world within the words of another (you couldn't prevent them from making these connections even if you tried!).

The types of questions students are asked influence how they read a text. If students are asked only recall and recitation questions, they learn to read for that type of information. If they are asked questions that require them to analyze, synthesize, and evaluate, they learn to read more closely and actively engage with the text. Unfortunately, many of the questions that students are asked are about personal connections, which may not even require them to have read the text at all. We are interested in questions that require students to locate evidence within the text. These text-dependent questions require a careful reading of the text such that students can produce evidence in their verbal or written responses. This is not to say that personal connections should be avoided at all costs. After all, readers naturally compare the information they are reading with their experiences. However, the argument for text-dependent questions asserts that discussions (and writing prompts) should focus on the text itself to build a strong foundation of knowledge. This purposefully built foundational knowledge can then be leveraged by learners to formulate opinions and make connections that are meaningful and informed.

As an example, consider the following two questions a teacher *could* ask of her students who have been studying an essay from *Last Call at the Oasis* (Weber, 2012) titled "A Way Forward? The Soft Path for Water" by Peter Gleick:

- Has your family made any changes to reduce water consumption?
- What are the differences between soft and hard paths to water management?

The first question can be answered without ever reading the essay. A conversation about the first question may be very animated and interesting, but it does not require that the students develop any level of understanding of the information presented by the author. If you were to observe this lesson, you might witness significant student engagement in a class discussion about the first question. But consider whether the actual text factored into the discussion or remained sitting on their desks unused. Accessing complex texts doesn't mean simply having them nearby— readers actually have to read them. Asking questions that require students to have to read and understood the text is crucial. The first question about family water consumption habits is actually irrelevant within the context of this essay, which focuses on systemic water conservation methods. It is important that as teachers we know how to engage students, beyond simply asking them to tell a personal story. The content itself can and should be used to engage.

The emphasis should be on getting students to use explicit and implicit information from the text to support their reasoning.

There are several ways to structure questions such that students return to the text to find evidence for their responses. We caution that these questions should not focus solely on recall. The emphasis should be on getting students to use explicit and implicit information from the text to support their reasoning. There are at least six categories of text-dependent questions that can be drawn from the standards and structured into a progression that will move students from understanding explicit meaning to understanding implicit meaning, and from working at the sentence level to working across an entire text and even with multiple texts. As well, some of these question types may not be suitable for a particular reading; there is no requirement that all of these types need to be used with every piece of text. Figure 3.2 contains a graphic of these questions. Further, as students discuss a given text, they will likely cover many of the questions that could have been asked. When they do so, the teacher does not need to ask a prepared question. We like to think of the prepared text-dependent questions as a resource that the teacher has to scaffold students' understanding and hope that much of the classroom conversation addresses the content of the question. The question samples below are based on the water essay referenced above. Examples of text-dependent questions for texts at the elementary grade levels can be found in Figure 3.3.

As noted in Figure 3.2, there are three overarching questions that we use to organize the flow of a close reading lesson. The lesson starts at the literal level, with the first two question types (general understanding and key details). Students should be thinking, "What does the text say?" When the

Figure 3.2 Text-Dependent Questions

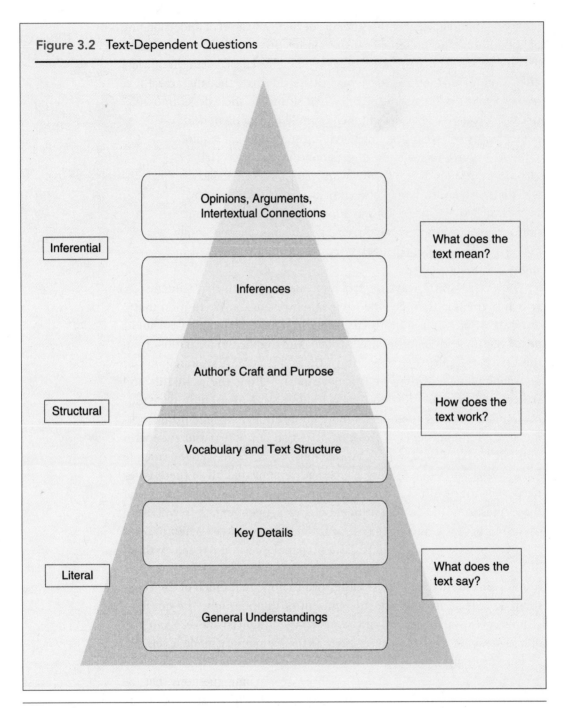

Figure 3.3 Sample Text-Dependent Questions

Question Type	Questions From *Frog and Toad Together* (Lobel, 1971) in First Grade	Questions From Chapter 10 in *A Night to Remember* (Lord, 1955) in Sixth Grade
General Understandings	Retell the story using *first, next, then,* and *finally.*	Why would the author title the chapter "Go Away"?
Key Details	What ways did they try to solve the problem of eating too many cookies?	What are two things that could have prevented this tragedy?
Vocabulary and Text Structure	How did the author help us to understand what *willpower* means?	How does the chronological structure help the reader understand the events?
Author's Craft and Purpose	Who tells the story?	Whose story is most represented and whose story is underrepresented?
Inferences	Do you think Toad's actions caused the seeds to grow? Why?	Why would Mrs. Brown run lifeboat number 6 with a revolver?
Opinions, Arguments, Intertextual Connections	In your opinion, is Frog a good friend to Toad? Do you think this is a happy story or a sad one?	Compare this book with *Inside the Titanic* (Brewster & Marschall, 1997). What are the similarities and differences?

Source: Fisher and Frey (2012a). © 2012. Reprinted by permission of the International Literacy Association, Newark, Delaware.

teacher has evidence that students have mastered the literal level of the text, the questions should shift to the structural level. Sometimes the teacher will have evidence from students' annotations that they understand the text at the literal level and thus should move on. Other times, the first literal question provides sufficient evidence of students' thinking. And still other times, the teacher will need to ask several literal questions to scaffold students' understanding of the text. Teachers should always have more literal questions ready than they probably need, because it's hard to predict when students will get stuck, and having questions ready prevents teachers from telling students what to think about the text.

Teachers should always have more literal questions ready than they probably need, because it's hard to predict when students will get stuck.

Following the literal level, the discussion and analysis moves to the structural level with the over-arching question of "How does the text work?" In this phase, the focus is on vocabulary, text structures, author's craft, and author's purpose. These are the choices that authors make as they construct a text. As readers explore the answers to these questions, the text becomes a mentor, and student writing will likely improve.

The final phase of the close reading focuses on the inferential level of understanding. This is where teachers want to get their students. But starting at this level can frustrate students and result in teachers telling students what to think. If the text is sufficiently complex, it won't give up its meaning easily, and the journey from literal to structural to inferential will scaffold students' understanding so that the teacher can guide the experience rather than directly explain the reading to students.

In the section that follows, we'll explore each of the question types that make up the three phases of a close reading lesson.

General Understandings

These questions get at the gist of the text. What does the author want us to know or understand from the text? Often, these questions focus on the main claim and the evidence used to support the claim or the arc of the story or the sequence of information. For the water essay, the teacher might ask,

"Which is the water path recommended by Gleick?"

Interestingly, this question is not directly addressed in the essay, and students will have to find clues from across the text to figure out his main claim. Alternatively, the teacher might direct students in this way:

"Discuss the ages of water and why Gleick believes we are headed into the third age."

As implied in the structure of this directive, text-dependent work does not need to take place solely in a whole-class setting. Students can be encouraged to discuss their thinking with their peers. This particular exercise will lead students to a more clear-cut answer, but the act of engaging in the discussion is central to getting them to understand the essay and the key point that the author is trying to make.

Key Details

These questions focus on asking students about the important details that the author uses to inform the reader. Often these questions include who, what, where, when, why, or how in the stem. They can also include reference to the more nuanced details that must be understood to add clarity to the reading. For example, the following question is key to understanding Gleick's perspective:

"What is the difference between water and water services?"

The teacher might also ask this:

"What is one method Gleick identifies for reducing water consumption?"

Key detail questions tend to focus on information presented directly in the text. Importantly, understanding this information should be critical to understanding the text; key detail questions should not focus simply on trivia. As well, these key details should be used to scaffold students' understanding as they respond to more complex questions.

Vocabulary and Text Structure

Some of the questions that students must consider revolve around the vocabulary used by the author, as well as the structure of the text itself. Text structure questions require that students consider the organization of the reading, such as the use of problem/solution or character dialogue to propel action. In asking questions related to vocabulary, teachers must be sure to make reference to both denotations (definitions)

If the text is sufficiently complex, it won't give up its meaning easily, and the journey from literal to structural to inferential will scaffold students' understanding so that the teacher can guide the experience.

and connotations (the ideas or feelings that a word invokes) of words. In addition, as appropriate, the questions may focus on shades of meaning, word choice, figurative language, idioms, and confusing words or phrases. Finally, questions can provide students an opportunity to use context or structural clues to determine the meaning of unknown words. For example, the teacher might ask students about the three key ideas discussed in the essay about water:

> "After reading this essay, how would you summarize the differences between productivity, efficiency, and supply?"

Alternatively, the teacher might ask students to determine the meaning of the word *ozonation* from the context clues or to discuss why the author chose the word *emerged* when talking about *Homo sapiens* over time. In addition, the teacher might ask students to comment on the structure of the essay and to note the differences between the parts in terms of tone and structure. Attentive students would notice those sections of the text with significant descriptions, with a reliance on problem/solution structures, and with a persuasive tone.

Author's Craft and Purpose

Inference questions require that students have read the entire selection so that they know where the text is going and how they can reconsider key points in the text as contributing elements of the whole.

The genre of the text and the use of narration help students make sense of what they are reading. So does the analysis of point of view and literary devices. On the flip side, understanding the overall purpose of the text guides students in following the flow of the reading. Readers should understand if the text is meant to inform, entertain, persuade, or explain something to them. There are also situations in which the text has a specific bias or provides only part of the story. In these situations, students could be asked about the perspectives not explored in the text. For the water essay, some examples of questions related to the author's purpose are as follows:

> "How does Gleick attempt to convince readers that water is a worthy issue of discussion?"

> "What is Gleick's purpose in writing this? Is he trying to inform, entertain, or persuade? How do you know?"

> "Is Gleick biased? What is your evidence?"

> "Does Gleick acknowledge other perspectives? If so, what is the effect? If not, how does that influence your reaction to the piece?"

Inferences

Some of the questions that students need to think about require that they understand how the parts of a text build to a whole. Unlike the cognitive processes associated with inference at the local level, these inferences require students to consider the piece as a whole. They probe each argument in persuasive text, each idea in informational text, or each key detail in literary text, and anchor them to the central themes of the piece. Importantly, inference questions require that students have read the entire selection so that they know where the text is going and how they can reconsider key points in the text as contributing elements of the whole. In the Gleick essay, students might be asked questions like these:

> "How does the information at the start of the essay, about the U.S. using less water today compared with 30 years ago, help Gleick make his argument for the third age of water?"

> "How does Gleick use the six differences between hard and soft paths to build the case for water services?"

Opinions, Arguments, and Intertextual Connections

The final category of text-dependent questions should be used sparingly, and typically comes after students have read, and reread, a text several times to fully develop their understanding. Readers should have opinions about what they read, and they should be able to argue their perspective using evidence from the text and other texts, experiences, and beliefs that they hold. For example, while reading about water, the teacher might ask questions like these:

> "Did Gleick make a convincing argument about the ages of water?"

> "Is there sufficient evidence presented that a soft path is the appropriate direction?"

> "How do Gleick's recommendations compare with those presented in the essay 'In Our Lifetime: Deconstructing the Global Water Crisis and Securing Safe Water for All' by Gary White?" (Weber, 2012)

These questions should result in deep and engaging conversations, especially when students have read and understood the text. Over time and with practice, students will begin asking themselves and their peers these types of questions, and the teacher will not be the only one who poses questions for discussion.

Annotation

In the last chapter, we recommended modeling annotation as a way to teach students how to interact with the text and how to interrupt the passive reading experience that can leave many of them struggling to find the meaning of a complex piece of text. Readers with a passive stance expect that the information will wash over them, and when it does not, they throw in the towel. Marking up the text allows them to witness their own growing understanding, and it encourages them to put into words what they do not yet understand. Annotation occurs first during their first or second pass at the text, but should also continue throughout subsequent discussion framed by text-dependent questions.

Readers with a passive stance expect that the information will wash over them.

For example, in an eighth-grade unit of study on adolescence, humanities teacher Paula Brown used several pieces of text that allowed her students to practice their annotation skills. She had previously modeled annotation with several other pieces of text, print and digital, and felt they were ready to begin using it themselves. As she told her students,

> Adolescence is a time when important decisions—some of them life changing—occur. It can be scary to think that some of the choices you make now can last a lifetime. In this unit of investigation, you will explore what a parent, a poet, and a psychologist have to say about making decisions that seem small at the time, but are big in hindsight. The purpose of this unit is to examine adolescent decision-making from three perspectives in order to locate central themes.

As part of this unit, students read and annotated an article titled "Psychologist Explains Teens' Risky Decision-Making Behavior" (Iowa State University, 2007). For example, a section of Javier's text was annotated in this way:

> Gerrard said that the initial risk-taking experience will influence an adolescent's intention to repeat the behavior in the future. They do consult their conscience over risk-taking, but not always in a classic "good vs. evil" way.

"From a kid's perspective, if you're operating in this more reasoned, thoughtful [experienced] mode—then you have the proverbial devil and the angel over your shoulder," she said. "If you're operating in the more experiential [impulsive] mode, you don't even know the angel is there. Those things are not in your mind at all, and the devil's only saying, 'This could be interesting.'" *EX*

After their first couple of readings through the text, Ms. Brown engaged students in a discussion using text-dependent questions, which encourage them to reread, and to consult their annotations, to deeply comprehend the passage. As part of their discussion, Ms. Brown asked students to consider the following questions, requiring that they provide evidence from the text for their responses:

- **General Understandings:** *What is the main finding of Dr. Gerrard's research?*
- **Key Details:** *What role does image play?*
- **Vocabulary and Text Structure:** *How did you figure out what* impulsive *and* reasoned *mean?*
- **Author's Craft and Purpose:** *Why is this genre appropriate for the content? Who is the intended audience for this article?*
- **Inferences:** *How can you determine that this is a credible source?*
- **Opinions, Arguments, and Intertextual Connections:** *Let's compare this article to the first reading we did ("Who's Right?"). How does this informational article explain some of the conflict occurring between mother and daughter?*

Marking up the text allows students to witness their own growing understanding, and it encourages them to put into words what they do not yet understand.

Throughout the discussion, the teacher reminded her students to mark up their text because "we read with our eyes, our brains, our hearts, and our pencils." She stated that the action of annotation gives them a sense of ownership and influence over the text and lowers the sense of intimidation that some readers feel when confronted with a difficult reading: "I want you to know that a reading shouldn't ever boss you around. I want you to see evidence of your growing understanding of the text as we get further into the discussion."

After-Reading Tasks

Rather than take students away from the text, post-reading activities should require them to return to the text. For example, students may write an argumentative piece in which they use evidence from the text. They may engage in a Socratic Seminar or debate a topic. After-reading tasks should help students consolidate the meaning of texts and deepen their comprehension far beyond what they would be able to accomplish on their own.

Having students create short written summaries of complex texts provides them with an opportunity to solidify their understanding and to develop a catalog of notes for comparing multiple pieces of text in the future. You will recall that Paula Brown's unit on adolescence included three pieces of text. She noted, "It's hard for them to make comparisons across documents when they don't have meaningful notes, so I often have them do some précis writing so they'll have useful writing to draw from later in the unit." Following their discussion on the article written by the psychologist, Ms. Brown asked her eighth-grade students to summarize their understanding of the text. She told her students, "Write a short summary of about 100 words that accurately summarizes the article. Be sure to include the name of the researcher and the findings. And remember to use your annotations to guide your writing."

As literacy educators, you have to ensure that students are engaged in reading texts that are worthy of their time.

Précis writings are summaries of a text or passage that require students to distill the main points but also involve them in the process of "selecting, rejecting, and paraphrasing ideas" (Bromley, 1985, p. 407). Teaching students how to compose précis writings develops their ability to understand the text more deeply and to learn essential content. These writing tasks do not contain the student's opinions or questions and should not include any information not discussed in the text itself. The students in Ms. Brown's class will later use these précis writings to produce a longer essay in which they address the topic of adolescent decision making from different perspectives.

Close readings are an important component of reading instruction, but they are not the only instructional routine that students need to experience to become successful readers. As literacy educators, you have to ensure that students are engaged in reading texts that are worthy of their time. You also have to ensure that students investigate the text sufficiently to really develop an appropriate level of understanding. Combined with shared, collaborative, and independent readings, close readings provide students the experiences they need to become skilled in analytic reading, a prerequisite for college and career success.

Close Reading for Young Readers

Thus far, the examples we have offered have involved older students, but if you are a primary teacher, you may be thinking, "How could this ever occur with my students?" K–3 students have an especially wide gap between the level of texts they can read on their own and those they can read with some adult support. In other words, they can understand narrative and informational texts that far outstrip their current reading levels. In most cases, the teacher is the reader of the text during a close reading lesson for students in the primary grades. Much of the literacy instruction during the primary grades focuses on foundational language skills, especially through scaffolded small-group, needs-based reading instruction as well as whole-class lessons on "grade-appropriate phonics and word-analysis skills to decode words accurately" as well as lessons that require students to "recognize and read with automaticity grade-level high frequency words." But close reading does something else for students in the primary grades: it develops their listening comprehension and thinking skills. At that age, students' listening comprehension far exceeds their reading comprehension. Close reading lessons allow students practice with comprehension skills while also practicing their listening, questioning, and sharing. One example is the use of *The Wonderful Wizard of Oz* (Baum, 1900/2000) in kindergarten. No one would expect five-year-olds to read this book on their own, or even with adult support. Rather, the intention is to expose young students to complex texts that challenge their thinking skills rather than their reading skills. Perhaps we should refer to this as *close listening*, because so much of this is about listening comprehension.

The intention is to expose young students to complex texts that challenge their thinking skills rather than their reading skills. Perhaps we should refer to this as close listening, *because so much of this is about listening comprehension.*

Read-alouds such as this should not be confused with the soothing after-lunch read-alouds teachers sometimes use. Being read aloud to plays an important role in reading for pleasure, and most of us have fond memories even decades later of read-aloud experiences such as this. We do not advocate that this practice be abandoned. However, we do advocate the addition of read-alouds that are designed to develop the critical thinking skills these students will use across their reading lives. We are referring to interactive read-alouds (Fisher, Flood, Lapp, & Frey, 2004) that require students to actively participate in the co-construction of knowledge and understanding in ways that are similar to the close readings described in the section above. Close listening (reading) lessons use an interactive think-aloud approach that draws from many of the same principles as those used for older students:

Video 3.5

Close reading in the primary grades.

resources.corwin.com/ rigorousreadingfla

- Uses short, worthy readings that are complex due to structure, use of language conventions, levels of meaning, or knowledge demand
- Requires the text to be reread several times throughout the lesson
- Frames discussion and deepens student understanding of the text through the use of text-dependent questions
- Relies on after-listening tasks that require students to draw on knowledge of the text

Figure 3.4 provides a comparison between close reading in the primary grades and lessons that are developed for older students.

Kindergarten teacher Mohamed Hassan uses readings from Aesop's fables to promote close listening. "These short tales are great for my kids during the first few months of school," he said. "They challenge them to really listen closely to get the details." He cited "The Lion and the Mouse" as an example.

"The version I use has some tough vocabulary in it, like *gnawed*, and *plight*, and *bound*," he said. "Great general academic words." He continued, "So I give them an introduction, really just a reminder about what we already know about how these fables work, so we're always looking for the moral of the story." The story is less than 200 words long, and after reading it to them twice, he fosters a discussion using text-based questions:

- **General Understandings:** *What happened? Tell me the story using your own words.*
- **Key Details:** *How did the lion help the mouse? How did the mouse help the lion?*
- **Vocabulary and Text Structure:** *What does the mouse mean when he says, "Perhaps I might be able to do you a turn one of these days?"* (Mr. Hassan said that he rereads the story again to them after posing this question.)
- **Author's Craft and Purpose:** *What is the moral of the story that Aesop wants us to know?*
- **Inferences:** *Why is the lion so surprised at the idea that a mouse could help him? What does the lion say and do that helps you answer this question?*

Figure 3.4 Comparing Close Reading in Primary and Upper Grades

Close Reading in Primary Grades	Elements	Close Reading in Upper Grades
The reading level of the text is significantly higher than students' reading level.	**Text Selection**	The text complexity is slightly higher than what the student takes on during other phases of reading instruction.
The teacher is reading the text aloud to students, although they are not grasping its deeper meaning. The text may or may not be displayed.	**Initial Reading**	Students are more likely to read the text independently, although they are not fully grasping its deeper meaning.
The teacher guides annotation practices using displayed text and fosters collaboratively developed annotations.	**Annotation**	Students familiar with annotation practices are marking the text independently and adding to their annotations throughout class discussions.
The teacher reads the text aloud multiple times. Students may read along at the paragraph, sentence, phrase, or individual word level. A few students may read the text independently in subsequent readings due to practice effects.	**Repeated Readings**	Students are rereading independently or with minimal support. Students may also have access to audio supports (a poet reading her poem, a teacher reading dialogue, a peer reading a key sentence).
Text-Based Discussions Students engage in extended discussion, which is driven by text-dependent questions and dialogic teaching. Students deepen their understanding through analysis of the literal, structural, and inferential dimensions of the text.		
Students draw and write collaboratively and independently, with adult support and guidance. They engage in shared investigations and debate compelling questions.	**Responding to Texts**	Students write collaboratively and independently. They investigate and research and debate compelling questions.

Mr. Hassan uses students' knowledge of the traditional telling of this tale, with its more difficult language structures, to introduce them to a wordless illustrated version of the story. "Sometimes I use an animation video with the sound turned off, and other times there is a print version available. Depends on the story," he added. In this case, he used Pinkney's (2009) *The Lion and the Mouse*. "Now they are retelling the story with each other using the illustrations, and it's amazing to hear them use more sophisticated language in their oral retellings because they know the original version so well," he said. "That use of oral language skills is so important in getting their reading off the ground."

While annotation isn't featured when using read-alouds, it can be a part of a shared reading experience that gives students visual exposure to the text. Poems on chart paper, projected readings, and texts that come in the form of big books all have a role in close reading in primary grade classrooms. Interactive SMART Boards have annotation features that are easily used by students, and low-tech items such as highlighting tape and reusable wax sticks work well in temporarily annotating large print items.

The first half of this chapter has been dedicated to close reading practices that guide students' understanding of complex texts. A key feature of this type of instruction is the use of text-dependent questions that draw students back into the reading. It's really the progression of the questions themselves that guides student thinking. But students are also developing their reading skills, and they need experiences with texts that are still complex but may not be as far up the proverbial staircase of complexity as the texts that are used in close reading. This needs-based practice, called *scaffolded reading instruction*, relies on questions, prompts, and cues to foster students' cognitive and metacognitive skills.

Students are developing their reading skills, and they need experiences with texts that are still complex but may not be as far up the proverbial staircase of complexity as the texts that are used in close reading.

▶ Accessing Complex Text Requires Scaffolded Reading Instruction

In scaffolded reading instruction, small groups of students with similar learning needs are grouped together for a short time to receive specific instruction from the teacher using text that will require instruction and support. These materials may include leveled texts for students in the primary grades (K–2) and complex texts, textbooks, or other readings the teacher has gathered for students in grades 3 and beyond. The purpose of scaffolded reading instruction is to deliver customized lessons based on recent assessment information. These assessments may be collected during the scaffolded reading instruction lesson itself or at other times during the day.

The major work of young readers is in melding foundational skills and comprehension skills to understand text. Consolidation of these skills is essential for emergent and early readers to master, and at times challenges with foundational skills, such as decoding, can impede their ability to fully access the text. Small-group scaffolded reading instruction is an ideal time to accomplish both.

First-grade teacher Alma Fernández uses small-group homogenous grouping to provide scaffolded reading instruction for four students she has gathered for customized phonics instruction that is tied to a text she will be using for shared reading. Based on her most recent assessment results, these students require additional attention. Her class will be reading *A Bike Like Sergio's* (Boelts, 2016) about a boy who faces a moral dilemma about whether to return money he found to the rightful owner or keep it for himself to purchase a bike. The text has complex concepts in it and will be a great story for prompting meaningful discussion. She previewed the first five pages of the text for her whole class yesterday afternoon, thinking aloud about the problem Ruben, the main character, will soon face. They are eager to dig into it today. However, Ms. Fernández knows that these students are having difficulty with initial and final consonant blends and digraphs. "They won't be reading the book entirely independently, but I don't want them to be tripped up with some of the phonics demands," she explains.

Ms. Fernández identified several such words featured in the book: *breath, wish, bread, blue, shuffle, float,* and *floor*. She has written these words on flashcards, and each child has a small magnetic whiteboard in front of them, in addition to blank index cards. She has also duplicated the first five pages of the story so that each child has a copy. The teacher introduces the words and tells the children that these words appear in the text they'll be reading together. For the next 15 minutes, Ms. Fernández moves her students through several phonics activities as they manipulate the words: constructing them with magnetic letters, isolating the blends and digraphs using the blank index cards as sliding doors to frame letters, fast-paced flashcard games, and writing some of the words themselves. Now, using the text, the children use colorful highlighters to mark the words they have been practicing. Finally, Ms. Fernández rereads the first five pages to them, pausing as she encounters a targeted word for them to supply. "This is a preview for them in advance of our reading this afternoon," she explains. "I'm always conscious of how important it is to tie decoding to comprehension," she continues, "so they can access the text meaningfully."

Scaffolded reading instruction typically lasts between 10 and 20 minutes, depending on the needs and stamina of the students. Stamina is a legitimate consideration for scaffolded reading instruction because this intensive instructional time may be the most cognitively demanding time of the day for students. In secondary classrooms, where instructional periods are far shorter than the 120 minutes allocated in elementary classrooms for reading instruction, a teacher may meet with only one group each period. However, these meetings are not limited to students who struggle with reading. In fact, all students benefit from this responsive instructional arrangement that allows the teacher to provide scaffolds with precision when needed and to withhold them when they are not necessary.

Scaffolded reading instruction can be used in secondary classes to guide collaborative reading groups. The students in Mike Sawyer's seventh-grade English class are organized in literature circles to read and discuss books related to the unit theme of Taking Responsibility. One group has selected *Stargirl* (Spinelli, 2003). Mr. Sawyer's observation of their last group meeting prompted him to meet with the five student members for additional scaffolded reading instruction. "They were stuck on condemning the students in the story who shunned Stargirl, but they weren't getting to a major understanding I had hoped would emerge by this point in the novel," he said. "They weren't really seeing that Stargirl's unorthodox character represented a part of what the others wished they could be but weren't brave enough to do."

Mr. Sawyer met with the group and asked them to reread the opening pages silently. "Sometimes there are these huge ideas that are represented at the very beginning, but we pass right over them because we don't know the story yet. As you read, can you find a line or two that is more meaningful to you now that you're nearly done with the book?" After a few minutes, Kendra offers, "Well, I'm not sure, but there's this line on page 2. 'It did not occur to me that I was being watched. We were all being watched.'" The teacher asks, "Why do you believe that's an overlooked gem?" and Kendra and the group engage in a conversation about self-consciousness and being observed. "I guess we get hung up on being worried more about what other people think," offers Jake.

"Now I'm going to ask you to make a big shift in the book, to chapter 9," says the teacher. "There's this extended passage about frogs that live in the mud in the desert," he continues. "Spinelli describes them as *dormant*.

How does the line in chapter 1 link to the discussion about frogs? I mean, who cares about frogs? But we know authors rarely put in details that have no usefulness." The group is silent at first, but then Troy ventures, "Maybe it's like everyone is hiding in the mud?" Kendra finishes his thought. "Like they're not really alive because they're too self-conscious?" His students have made an important conceptual shift as they begin to understand more fully why the shunning has occurred. "So they're not bad people, like evil," says Troy. "But they're afraid, and not really awake to who they really are," adds Antonio. The teacher smiles, as he senses that the next literature circle discussion will be enriched because of the time he spent with them in scaffolded instruction. "Sometimes it's just the catalyst they need to make these big leaps in understanding," said Mr. Sawyer.

In the following section, we will describe in more detail the principles and practices that guide effective scaffolded reading instruction:

- The student, not the teacher, is the reader.
- Small groups help differentiate support.
- Students have similar strengths and needs.
- Grouping patterns change frequently.
- Using questions and providing prompts and cues guide learners.

We will also discuss why *whole-class* scaffolded reading instruction creates difficulties.

The Student, Not the Teacher, Is the Reader

Everything in a scaffolded reading instruction lesson is designed to lead to the student reading the text. Often, this is accomplished through silent reading. The teacher may designate stop points in the text so the group can discuss the reading and clarify misunderstandings. Not surprisingly, this is not realistic with emergent readers who do not read silently, or with early readers who are just beginning to do so. Therefore, it can be tempting to have each student take a turn and publicly read a portion of the text. This practice, called *round robin reading*, is an ineffective and potentially detrimental approach to reading instruction (Optiz & Rasinski, 2008).

Another practice, called *choral reading*, refers to the practice of having students read in unison. Choral reading can be an effective tool for building

It can be tempting to have each student take a turn and publicly read a portion of the text. This practice, called round robin reading, *is an ineffective and potentially detrimental approach to reading instruction.*

fluency through repeated readings, especially in reader's theater. It is also an appropriate strategy for dramatic performances such as the recitation of a poem. Its usefulness is limited in scaffolded reading instruction, however, because the purpose here is to provide more individualized support for students. There may be brief passages that lend themselves to choral reading, particularly alliterative sentences or rhyming passages that beg to be heard aloud. That said, the student-reading portion of the scaffolded reading instruction lesson should be devoted to the individual.

Small Groups Help Differentiate Support

The purpose of holding scaffolded reading instruction groups to no more than six is to ensure that the teacher can provide more direct contact time with each learner. When group sizes grow beyond this number, management demands may take precedence over instruction. In addition, the small size of the group allows the teacher to observe each student up close in the act of learning. Insight into a learner's problem-solving skills can inform future instruction because the teacher gains an understanding of what the students do when they get to a "tricky part."

Although the group should not exceed six, it is acceptable for it to be as small as one student. This is especially true when working with students who significantly struggle with reading. While it may be tempting to place all the lowest-achieving students in one group, it is likely that they require more individualized instruction than their grade-level peers because their skill profiles are more idiosyncratic. In our experience, normally progressing readers tend to have a great deal in common with one another, whereas those who struggle tend to be unique in their patterns of strength and areas of need.

As we will discuss in the next chapter, the students who are not with the teacher in scaffolded reading instruction can be collaborating with their peers or working independently. Scaffolded reading instruction should not result in hours of independent work for the rest of the class.

Students Have Similar Strengths and Needs

Most commonly, teachers form scaffolded reading instruction groups based on similar literacy strengths and needs, called a *homogeneous group*. This is done for two reasons: practicality and peer support. It is practical because the teaching day simply does not have enough minutes in it to allow for individual instruction for each student. Small-group structures also capitalize on the power of peer influence on learning. Stated another

Video 3.6

Teacher works with groups of students to facilitate their understanding.
resources.corwin.com/ rigorousreadingfla

way, students benefit from the questions and insights of their peers in a teacher-directed group.

Grouping Patterns Change Frequently

We have stated that students are grouped based on a number of considerations, especially student strengths and needs. It is also vital to remember that these grouping patterns should not be static. In other words, the scaffolded reading instruction group a child belongs to in September should not be composed of the same classmates in May. It is essential for students to benefit from numerous opportunities to learn with one another; flexible grouping patterns ensure this happens. It is equally critical that students see themselves as contributors to the learning of others; flexible grouping patterns ensure this happens as well. Of course, careful consideration about how students are grouped is only a small part of scaffolded reading instruction. These groups are formed to implement powerful forms of teaching in which questions, prompts, and cues are used to provide students access to complex texts.

Using Questions and Providing Prompts and Cues Guide Learners

Students need experiences with a range of complex texts—not just the ones highlighted for close reading, which are quite complex. During scaffolded reading instruction, teachers provide more support and guidance than they do during close reading. This requires a teacher who can listen carefully to what students are saying to give them just enough support to let them find the answer. At the heart of scaffolded reading instruction lies the strategic use of questions to check for understanding, prompts to trigger cognitive and metacognitive thinking, and cues as needed to shift attention more overtly (Fisher & Frey, 2010b). In other words, rather than relying on text-dependent questions and repeated reading for the scaffolds—as is the case in close reading—the teacher provides support by attending to the misconceptions and errors that students make. Scaffolded reading instruction also provides students with practice applying comprehension strategies while learning to resolve their confusions.

Video 3.7

Teacher uses prompts and cues to guide learning.
resources.corwin.com/ rigorousreadingfla

Questions to Check for Understanding

The subject of questioning is critical to scaffolded reading instruction because questioning is the very core of the instruction. Once students have finished the reading for the lesson, teachers should pose literal and inferential questions to them. Retelling is a query at the *literal* level and is closely

It is useful to prepare literal and inferential questions to begin meaningful discussion with students.

associated with comprehension. Teachers should invite students to retell and encourage them to use their books to support their retelling. Readers should return to the text as needed, and this should be considered an acceptable classroom practice. For instance, asking how the Big Bad Wolf disguised himself in *Little Red Riding Hood* is an example of a literal question.

In addition, ask questions that require students to *infer* meaning about the text, such as questions that ask about the main idea, or about the author's purpose for writing the book. An example of an inferential question for the same book is inquiring about why the wolf chose to disguise himself as an old woman and not a young man. Questioning may also probe students' reactions and opinions of the text. Asking a reader about his or her thoughts concerning talking to strangers encourages students to form an opinion and to provide evidence for their responses. Although every question you may ask cannot be anticipated in advance, it is useful to prepare literal and inferential questions to begin meaningful discussion with students.

Scaffolded reading instruction begins when the teacher poses a question to check for understanding. This is not the time to assess students but rather a time to uncover misconceptions or errors. Students should be asked a variety of questions to check their understanding, and teachers should be continually on the lookout for misconceptions and errors.

For example, when Meghan Becovic asked a group of students to explain how they knew if something was living, she wanted to uncover their understanding of the scientific definition of life, a concept they had been reading about. When her students provided her with a number of correct responses, she changed direction asking, "So is evolution a characteristic of life?" When several students nodded positively, she knew that she had uncovered a misconception that she needed to address. There are a number of question types useful in checking for understanding, such as *clarifying* and *elaboration* questions in which students are encouraged to add details and examples to their answers. When students are asked to clarify or elaborate on their responses, misconceptions, errors, and partial understandings will reveal themselves.

Prompts for Cognitive or Metacognitive Work

When errors or misconceptions are identified, the first step in resolving them is to prompt the student to engage in mental work, either cognitive or metacognitive. Unfortunately, in too many classrooms, when errors

Video 3.8

Teacher uses questioning techniques to aid student comprehension.
resources.corwin.com/rigorousreadingfla

Video 3.9

Teacher works with small groups of students to generate questions.
resources.corwin.com/rigorousreadingfla

are identified, teachers skip the prompts and cues and instead provide the missing information for students. In this case, the student has not done any of the work and likely did not learn anything from the exchange. Teachers can prompt students' background knowledge and experiences, the rules they have been taught, or the procedures commonly used to solve problems (Figure 3.5 contains a list of common prompts used during scaffolded reading instruction). For example, when Frank Acerno questioned his students about a science article they were reading, he uncovered a misconception about speed versus velocity. In prompting them, he asked, "Remember the animation we watched about driving to school? Velocity and speed have some things in common, but . . ." The students immediately responded with a quote from the animation, "velocity is speed with direction," and their misconception was resolved.

When students are asked to clarify or elaborate on their responses, misconceptions, errors, and partial understandings will reveal themselves.

Cues to Shift Attention

If prompts fail to resolve the error or misconception, teachers can assume a more directive role through the use of cues. Cues should shift students' attention to something they've missed or overlooked (Figure 3.6 contains a list of common cues used during scaffolded reading instruction). A simple cue might be, "Take a look at the figure on page 112. Does that help?" There are a number of cues that are effective, including gestural, verbal, visual, physical, environmental, and positional. Of course, teachers use these cues regularly in their initial teaching, but often fail to use them when students are stuck. While reading an article on migration during the U.S. westward expansion, Terri Goetz identified an error that was not resolved through prompting. She used her voice and a gesture to shift students' attention. While pointing to a graph, she said, "Population PER thousand," emphasizing the word *per* with her voice.

Direct Explanations

Sometimes, prompts and cues do not resolve the errors or misconceptions that students have. In those cases, students cannot be left hanging. Teachers must ensure that students have a successful learning experience, even if that means providing a direct explanation and giving the student the answer. Importantly, direct explanations should come after prompts and cues to increase the likelihood that students can connect this new information to a thinking process in which they were engaged.

Figure 3.5 Types of Prompts

Type of Prompt	Definition/When to Use	Examples
Background knowledge	Used when there is content that the student already knows, has been taught, or has experienced but has temporarily forgotten or is using incorrectly.	• As part of a science passage about the water cycle, the teacher asks, "What do you remember about states of matter?" • When reading about a trip to the zoo, the teacher asks, "Remember when we had a field trip to the zoo last month? Do you recall how we felt when it started to rain?"
Process or procedure	Used when established or generally agreed-on rules or guidelines are not being followed and a reminder will help resolve the error or misconception.	• The student is saying a word incorrectly, and the teacher says, "When two vowels go walking. . . ." • When the student has difficulty starting to develop a writing outline, the teacher says, "I'm thinking about the mnemonic we've used for organizing an explanatory article."
Reflective	Used to encourage students to be metacognitive and to think about their thinking, which can then be used to determine next steps or the solution to a problem.	• The student has just read something incorrectly, and the teacher asks, "Does that make sense? Really think about it." • When the student fails to include evidence in her writing, the teacher asks, "What are we learning today? What was our purpose?"
Heuristic	Used to help learners develop their own way to solve problems. These are informal problem-solving procedures. They do not have to be the same as others' heuristics, but they do need to work.	• When the student has difficulty explaining the relationships between characters in a text, the teacher says, "Maybe drawing a visual representation of the main character's connections to one another will help you." • When a student gets stuck and cannot think of what to write next, the teacher says, "Writers have a lot of different ways for getting unstuck. Some just write whatever comes to mind, others create a visual, others talk it out with a reader, and others take a break and walk around for a few minutes. Will any of those help you?"

Source: **Adapted from Fisher and Frey (2013a). Used with permission of ASCD.**

Figure 3.6 Types of Cues

Type of Cue	Definition	Example
Visual	A range of graphic hints that guide students through thinking or understanding.	• Highlighting places on a text where students have made errors • Creating a graphic organizer to arrange content visually • Asking students to take a second look at a graphic or visual from a textbook
Verbal	Variations in speech used to draw attention to something specific or verbal attention getters that focuses students' thinking.	• "This is important . . ." • "This is the tricky part. Be careful and be sure to . . ." • Repeating a student's statement using a questioning intonation • Changing volume or speed of speech for emphasis
Gestural	Teacher's body movements or motions used to draw attention to something that has been missed.	• Pointing to the word wall when a student is searching for the right word or the spelling of a word • Making a hand motion that has been taught in advance such as one used to indicate the importance of summarizing or predicting while reading • Placing thumbs around a key idea in a text that the student was missing
Environmental	Using the surroundings, and things in the surroundings, to influence students' understanding.	• Keeping environmental print current so that students can use it as a reference • Using magnetic letters or other manipulatives to guide students' thinking • Moving an object or person so that the orientation changes and guides thinking

Source: Adapted from Fisher and Frey (2013a). Used with permission of ASCD.

Following the direct explanation, the teacher should monitor students' understanding by asking them to repeat the information back in their own words or asking the original checking for understanding question again. In this way, students are accountable for the information and for processing the experience with their teacher.

The Trouble With Whole-Class Scaffolded Reading Instruction

The process we outlined above works best with small groups of students. It's a difficult process to put into place in a whole-class setting. While checking for understanding can be done effectively with the whole class, when the teacher moves to prompt or cue, some students disengage. Some students don't need the information that their teacher is providing right now, either because it's not relevant or because they already understand the concept. When some students disengage, they distract others. Improving classroom management, however, won't improve this situation. Unless scaffolded reading instruction is done quickly and expertly and all of the students have a task to do while the teacher prompts and cues those who need it, some students will lose focus. It's just human nature. It's better to address misconceptions or errors with small groups of students or individually, especially while students work collaboratively or independently.

When the teacher moves to prompt or cue, some students disengage.

Returning to the life science teacher, Meghan Becovic, and the students' misunderstanding of the definition of living, prompts and cues were used to ensure their eventual understanding. At one point, Ms. Becovic asked her students to identify the characteristics all living things share. Part of their conversation follows:

Jamal:	One thing for life is breathing.
Teacher:	Do all things breathe? Think about that.
Mubarik:	Yes. We have to breathe or die.
Teacher:	So, I'm thinking about plankton.
Anais:	No, some things don't breathe.
Mubarik:	Oh, yeah, I forgot. But there is a word for what I'm thinking.
Jamal:	Is it metabolism?
Mubarik:	Yeah, that's it. To be alive you have to have metabolism.
Anais:	Yeah, that was in the book. I remember now.

Teacher:	Is metabolism the same as evolution?
Jamal:	No, but living things have to evolve or die.
Anais:	Wait a minute. We said that before, that they will die.
Teacher:	Take a look on this page [pointing to a website displayed on a computer].
Mubarik:	It says that living things have to reproduce. It doesn't say nothing about evolution.
Jamal:	So, maybe things don't have to evolve to be alive. Maybe that's more long term, not if the thing is alive right now.

As their conversation continued, the students in this group reached greater understanding of the content because their teacher did not simply tell them the missing information but rather scaffolded their understanding through prompts and cues. We have to be sure we provide this type of support for students who are stuck. When this is not provided, students become dependent on adults for information. When this support is provided, students become independent thinkers and learners who thrive inside and outside of the classroom.

▶ Summary

Close reading and scaffolded reading instruction establish critical access points to complex texts because they begin the shift of responsibility to the learner. Through the process of close reading, students are learning to stay close to the text to gain knowledge. These close reading lessons can be done in whole-group or small-group settings, and it is the text itself that is the predominant source of information. But students are also acquiring the skills of reading, and they need practice in drawing on their own cognitive and metacognitive resources as they read. This is achieved through scaffolded reading and requires the teacher to offer supports that encourage students to use what they already know as well as what the text has to offer.

iStock.com/imtmphoto

Access Point Three

Collaborative Conversations

Four sixth-grade students are deeply involved in a discussion about the book they are reading in their literature circle, *The Music of Dolphins* (Hesse, 1996). The story centers on a young girl who has been raised in warm Caribbean waters by a school of dolphins. Named Mila by her rescuers, she is brought to a facility to be studied by scientists who are interested in the language development of feral children. However, Mila hopes to escape this bewildering environment and return to the only family she has ever known.

David opens the conversation. "In chapter 53, Mila begs Doctor Beck to let her go back to the ocean, but the doctor says she can't because she will go to prison. What did all of you think about that?"

"I think Mila said it best on page 163—'I look at her. I am already in prison.' Mila feels trapped, like she's suffocating," offers Estefany.

Marisol holds up her notebook for everyone to see.

> That sentence meant a lot to me, too. I drew a picture of a
> girl in a cage at the zoo as I read that. I was remembering

Video 4.1

Teacher
introduces
literature circles.
*resources.corwin.com/
rigorousreadingfla*

her conversation with her friend Justin, when he asked her if she got tired of people coming to look at her all the time.

David asks another question when the group gets quiet. "Reynaldo, do you have an idea to add?" At this, Reynaldo responds,

> Well, I wrote this in my notebook: "Mila feels like she's just a thing, not a person, and that nobody except for Justin even tries to see her as anything more than a dolphin girl. It feels that way in school sometimes, when everyone is checking everyone else out and deciding whether they're cool or not. It's like no one even bothers to look past your clothes or hair or where you live."

These students are participating in a collaborative learning format called *literature circles* (Daniels, 2002). In between meetings, they read independently and make notes in their notebooks to be used in the next discussion. Each meeting is moderated entirely by the students themselves, who determine the direction of the conversation and the next reading task. In this way, students collaborate with one another to access complex texts.

Collaborative learning is one of the critical linchpins through which students access complex text because it enables them to consolidate their understanding with peers and provide support for one another in the absence of the teacher. We use the term *collaborative learning* in reference to work done with peers. These peer-assisted learning opportunities furnish students with a means of applying the skills and strategies they have learned during modeling, close reading, or scaffolded instruction. Collaborative conversations are a vital facet of group learning.

▶ Accessing Complex Texts Requires Collaborative Conversations

Increasing the amount of time students talk using academic language has been a priority for decades (see Fisher, Frey, & Rothenberg, 2008, for a review). Simply said, students need practice with academic language if they are to become proficient in that language. We don't only mean in English class; students must learn to speak the language of science, history, mathematics, art, literature, and technical subjects if they are to become thinkers in those disciplines (Fang, 2012).

From the time that there have been educational standards, speaking and listening have been included. In other words, this is not new. What is new is the role that student-to-student interaction plays in the standards. Although there is a great deal of attention paid to the reading and writing standards, we believe that educators should also attend to the increased demands placed on the speaking and listening domain, especially given the expectation that Florida students across the grade levels "use appropriate collaborative techniques and active listening skills when engaging in discussions in a variety of situations" (Florida Department of Education, 2020, p. 147). The Florida B.E.S.T. Standards do not provide specifics for grade levels, but the fact that this is a universal expectation speaks to the importance of speaking and listening.

Video 4.2

Teaching students to collaborate.
resources.corwin.com/rigorousreadingfla

There is no reading gene that is passed from one generation to the next. Each and every brain must be taught to read anew. Unlike hair or eye color that is transmitted from one generation to the next, reading is a complex, rule-based system that must be imposed on biological structures that were designed or evolved for other reasons (Wolf, 2007). Although most children are born with the right structures, these structures don't inherently know how to read. These structures are hardwired to speak and listen. In other words, we were born to talk (Hulit, Howard, & Fahey, 2010). Reading and writing are optional accessories that are bolted onto a speaking and listening brain.

Decades of research, not to mention personal experiences, confirms that listening comprehension outpaces reading comprehension from early childhood through at least middle school. Based on their review of research, Stricht and James (1984) analyzed the gap between listening and reading comprehension by age of learner (see Figure 4.1). What is obvious from this figure is the fact that access to complex ideas, for many years of the learner's life, requires oral rather than written input. Simply stated, children can listen to, and talk about, much more complex ideas than they can read (and probably write) about. In addition to the research, anyone who has ever read a bedtime story to a preschooler knows that listening comprehension is more sophisticated than reading comprehension. The proof comes from nights when you're tired and you skip a page while reading a bedtime story. That 3-, 4-, or 5-year-old's eyes pop open. You are accused of skipping a page, and the punishment is now that you must start over. Yes, in fact, they are listening, understanding, and comparing the text with their expectations. What is less obvious from personal experience is the persistence of this gap. According to Stricht and James, the gap extends well into middle school. This gap has implications for high-quality instruction across the learner's elementary and middle school experience, and oral language development should not be considered solely the role and responsibility of early childhood educators.

Students need practice with academic language if they are to become proficient in that language.

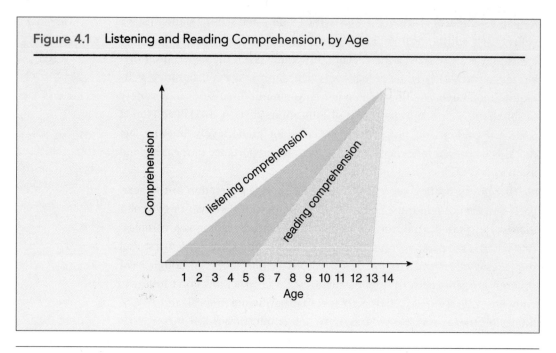

Figure 4.1   Listening and Reading Comprehension, by Age

Source: **National Governors Association (2010).**

In this time of great interest of increasing text complexity, the data represented in the figure raised several questions for us. Is it possible that one way to ensure that students read at increasingly sophisticated levels is to focus on increasing their listening comprehension? In other words, if we pushed listening comprehension higher than identified in the previous research, would reading comprehension follow? If we did so, would it take longer to close the gap or would the gap size remain, although at a higher level? If we want to ensure that students read increasingly complex information texts, it seems logical that students should be talking during their content area learning (e.g., Nystrand & Gamoran, 1991). As Biemiller notes, "Oral comprehension sets the ceiling on reading comprehension." Britton said it another way: "Reading and writing float on a sea of talk." In other words, as students' listening comprehension improves, so does their potential for reading comprehension. That's why collaborative conversations are an access point to complex texts.

For collaborative learning to work, teachers must structure the time students have to interact with their peers to work toward these new skills. We will limit our conversation about collaborative learning to those structures and habits that provide students increased access to complex texts. There are a host of collaborative learning routines that provide this type of access, and some that are useful in other ways. That said, it is important to recognize that students must be taught to collaborate with their peers.

Building Structures for Collaborative Learning

"I'm just not sure they're really doing anything of value when they're in groups."

This is perhaps the most frequent reservation we hear from educators when the subject of student collaboration comes up. Worried about the amount of instructional time dedicated to a group project, some teachers question whether it is better to simply tell students what they need to know. But telling alone isn't especially effective. Other teachers possess a fixed idea about the task itself, believing incorrectly that for the work to be worthwhile, it must extend over several class periods. Still others express concerns about individual students who prefer to work alone rather than in a group. Armed with these misgivings, many teachers list the benefits of group work, and then offer an apology: "It just doesn't work for the students I teach."

These apprehensions prevent otherwise innovative educators from deepening their instructional practices. And many of these qualms are rooted in the potential issues surrounding task complexity. Some teachers worry about logistic and behavior problems if the task is too easy or too difficult. They question the value of the learning itself, wondering aloud whether it's worth the fuss. And, at times, they may even question whether their students are capable of sustained group work without the constant presence of an adult. Addressing *task* complexity is key to ensuring that the time devoted to productive group work is in fact productive (Frey, Fisher, & Everlove, 2009). Quality indicators of appropriate task complexity take the following factors into account:

We suggest that teachers post, teach, and revisit norms for interaction, especially those that explain how to debate and disagree without being disagreeable, and how to seek, offer, accept, and decline help graciously.

- Designs that require students to work together
- Structures that elevate academic language
- The presence of grade level work
- The opportunity for productive failure

Designs That Require Students to Work Together

Group tasks require the same sort of thoughtful design process that goes into other aspects of instruction. First and foremost, students need to know how to interact with one another and how to seek help. We have sometimes heard teachers remark that they shouldn't have to teach about the norms of interaction, as "students should know how to work with each other by now." This is true, but only to a point. While students may have ample experience with group work in previous grades, they don't yet know how to work *for you*. Therefore, we suggest that teachers post, teach, and revisit norms for interaction, especially those that explain how to debate and disagree without being disagreeable, and how to seek, offer, accept, and decline help graciously.

It is important that teachers keep task complexity in mind when introducing new routines to students. Students who are learning a new way to work with one another should not be challenged with demanding content at the same time. The task complexity itself should be temporarily lowered to make it possible for students to attend to the collaborative learning processes and procedures that are new to them.

Structures That Elevate Academic Language

Video 4.4

Teacher outlines expectations, especially for language usage.
resources.corwin.com/ rigorousreadingfla

Students also need to know how to use the academic language of the lesson. Students of any age or level of experience benefit from language scaffolds that encourage them to use academic language and vocabulary. The use of language frames (partially constructed statements and questions that frame original ideas) is highly effective during collaborative conversations. In particular, teachers may find that students need sentence starters as they get used to using argumentation in their discussions. These language frames can be posted on table tents or on chart paper. For example, Karen Jessop provided her students with the following frames when they wanted to offer a counter claim:

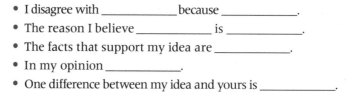

- I disagree with _____ because _____.
- The reason I believe _____ is _____.
- The facts that support my idea are _____.
- In my opinion _____.
- One difference between my idea and yours is _____.

Ensure Grade-Level Work

When students are engaged in productive group work, the expected level of rigor for a given task should be made clear. It really doesn't matter how good the instruction is if students in a fifth-grade class are working on third-grade-level content. The result is predictable—the students will have learned third-grade information, not fifth-grade information. Although we understand that there are students who currently perform below grade level, lowering expectations is not the way to close the achievement gap. Some students require scaffolded reading instruction, which involves the teacher using questions, prompts, cues, and direct explanations. As we noted in the previous chapter, students can be grouped based on assessed needs, and the teacher can focus on those needs with small groups. Other students require supplemental or intensive intervention, which is the focus of the Response to Intervention efforts under way in most districts (Fisher & Frey, 2010a). Importantly, while students are working productively with their peers and have peer support and language brokers, they should be working on tasks and texts that facilitate their understanding of grade-level concepts. The texts that are used in collaborative conversations and peer learning should be suitably complex for where the students are within the school year. Keep in mind that the collective work of the group is to make meaning together, and, accordingly, the texts used can and should be more complex than those texts students have used in their independent reading.

That's what collaborative learning should do: It should provide students with an opportunity to consolidate their understanding of rigorous concepts so that they can access increasingly complex texts.

Consider a task Mr. Bonine's life science students completed as part of their unit on energy in an ecosystem. Each group of students was provided an envelope that contained little slips of paper with words on them. The words on the slips of paper were terms for different organisms in an ecosystem. Students were asked to sort the words in any categorical system that made sense to them. As group members moved words into categories, they had to defend their placement to their peers. They were encouraged to use a language frame, "This organism, _____, belongs in the _____ category because _____." When Imani moved the paper with the word *bacteria* to a new column, she said, "This organism, bacteria, belongs in a new category because it doesn't fit in any of these others." Her team members agreed, putting their thumbs up to show their agreement.

Once students had their categories, Mr. Bonine introduced technical vocabulary, including the terms *autotroph* and *heterotroph*. He asked students to re-sort their organisms based on this new information. Spenser moved all of the words back to a pile, saying, "These categories of predator and prey don't work for this. This organism, zooplankton, belongs in the heterotroph category because it can't make organic compounds. Instead, it eats other organisms."

During the period, Mr. Bonine added additional terms, such as *decomposer* and *producer*, and asked his students to continue their sorts. In doing so, the students in this biology class completed tasks designed to ensure their learning of grade-level biology concepts. He then moved them into a complex reading on these concepts, a science piece on the use of heterotrophs for recycling and biodiesel production, and students met in small groups to

Video 4.5

Students work collaboratively on a presentation.
resources.corwin.com/ rigorousreadingfla

discuss the article. And that's what collaborative learning should do: It should provide students with an opportunity to consolidate their understanding of rigorous concepts so that they can access increasingly complex texts.

Design for Productive Failure

"Failure" may seem antithetical to education, but we consider its presence a quality indicator of task complexity. In much the same way that we recognize that we often learn from our mistakes, so it is with the learners in our classrooms. The growing research on productive failure in learning is that students who initially fail at a task are more receptive to subsequent instruction, as evidenced by increased achievement and performance (Kapur, 2008). Importantly, we don't want students to experience this failure in isolation. The best time for them to do so is during collaborative learning.

Collaborative learning isn't just pushing desks together and then calling it a day. Collaborative learning hinges on the complexity of a given task and the degree to which students cognitively engage with it.

A task designed with the possibility of productive failure in mind must be one that is sufficiently novel. In other words, it should not be a mere reproduction of what the teacher just did. A problem with reproductive tasks is that they are susceptible to the "divide and conquer" or the parallel independent work approaches in which so many groups engage. In these scenarios, the task itself is already known; now it's just a matter of students following the steps—no thinking required. Groups with this mindset merely divide up the task, go their separate ways, and then get back together to assemble the final product.

For the task to possess the possibility of productive failure, it must also be designed to require interaction and teamwork. The text students are using should be complex enough that they actually need each other to broker an understanding of it. It is important to listen in on a group that is wrestling with a text that is difficult enough to possibly fail. In doing so, you'll likely hear students discussing the content, not just the task. They will use academic language and vocabulary in ways that indicate they are cognitively engaging with the topic. Ideally, they will also ask questions of one another, offer explanations and clarifications, and provide evidence to support their claims. To be sure, making this quality indicator a reality in your classroom requires getting close to groups to hear how they apply their knowledge to solve problems. But this is essential to more fully understanding the quality of learning that is occurring in your classroom.

Collaborative learning work isn't just pushing four desks together and then calling it a day. A truer measure of the value of collaborative learning hinges on the complexity of a given task and the degree to which students cognitively engage with it. The complexity of the task ensures they have something to talk about; the structure of the task provides them the forum for doing so.

Key Elements of Collaborative Learning

Although there is a strong research base on the effectiveness of peer-assisted learning that takes place in cooperative and collaborative groups, it is also widely recognized that it is challenging to implement the kinds of grouping scenarios that give rise to this learning. Like all good instruction, collaborative learning requires careful planning to ensure success for teachers and students. We have included a checklist in Figure 4.2 for you to use as you consider the key elements of the planning process. Below, we will discuss in more detail those related to grouping, goal setting, and the accountability measures.

Grouping

One of the first decisions a teacher must make when using collaborative learning has to do with how to pair or group students. Should the groups be composed of students working at a similar level (homogeneous grouping) or of differing levels (heterogeneous)? Effective teachers tell us that when they are making grouping decisions, they consider how the group might receive help when faced with a difficult task. In teacher-directed groups such as scaffolded reading instruction, that help is available in the form of the teacher because he or she is working with students at the time. However, in collaborative learning, the students are working apart from the teacher, and help is not as easily obtained. Therefore, the help must emerge from within the group. This help is more likely to occur in mixed-ability pairs or groups. This advantage of mixed-ability groups has been articulated in student feedback as well. In a study of grouping preferences of more than 500 elementary schoolchildren, Elbaum, Schumm, and Vaughn (1997) reported that students preferred mixed-ability groups (especially pairs) to homogeneous groups. On a related note, Bennett and Cass (1989) found that having specific ratios of students with particular ability levels was also important to heterogeneous groups. They noted that the optimal group was composed of two lower-performing students and one higher-performing student. In groups where the ratio was reversed (two higher-performing students to one lower-performing one), the lone struggling student was often left out of the activities. It is interesting to note that the higher-achieving students performed equally well in both circumstances.

Effective teachers tell us that when they are making grouping decisions, they consider how the group might receive help when faced with a difficult task.

Video 4.6

Reciprocal teaching: predict and question.
resources.corwin.com/ rigorousreadingfla

Figure 4.2 Planning Checklist for Collaborative Learning

❏ What text will students be using?

❏ What are my learning intentions for the group?

- Academic

- Social

❏ What is the task?

❏ Where do the groups fit into my instructional sequence?

❏ What accountability measures will be used?

- Group accountability

- Individual accountability

Goal Setting

Successful collaborative learning pairs or groups understand what their goals are for the task at hand. Be sure to give groups specific directions concerning the task. For example, if they are working together to analyze the structure of an argument put forward by an author, provide them with a rubric describing what you're looking for in the final product that they will be producing. Younger children can benefit from task cards that describe each step in detail. Many students benefit from timelines as well. Multi-step tasks can be broken down into units of time to give a pair or group another way of monitoring their progress.

Accountability

A common criticism of collaborative learning is that the distribution of labor may be uneven. However, this can only occur when there is a flawed accountability system in place. Authorities on this type of instructional arrangement recommend both group and individual accountability measures (Johnson, Johnson, Holubec, & Roy, 1984). This means that student learning should ideally be measured in two ways: first, through a group assessment linked to the completion of the task, and second, through an individual assessment designed to gauge each student's contributions to the effort. Considerations about how you will measure individual accountability should be taken into account when you are building the task itself. Below are some structures for collaborative work that can provide built-in accountability measures.

- **A collaborative poster:** The teacher might assign each member of a group a different colored marker to use in the development of a collaborative poster. In this way, the different colors serve as evidence of each member's contributions.
- **Literature circles:** In literature circles, students' notes typically highlight each member's contributions. It is also common, for instance, to use assigned roles when students are first learning the literature circle format (e.g., the discussion director, vocabulary enricher, etc.). The notes students create during their literature circle meeting can be organized to mirror the roles they are using. As the groups become more proficient, the distinction between the roles can be faded.

> *A common criticism of collaborative learning is that the distribution of labor may be uneven. However, this can only occur when there is a flawed accountability system.*

Video 4.7

Students collaborate to learn content.
resources.corwin.com/ rigorousreadingfla

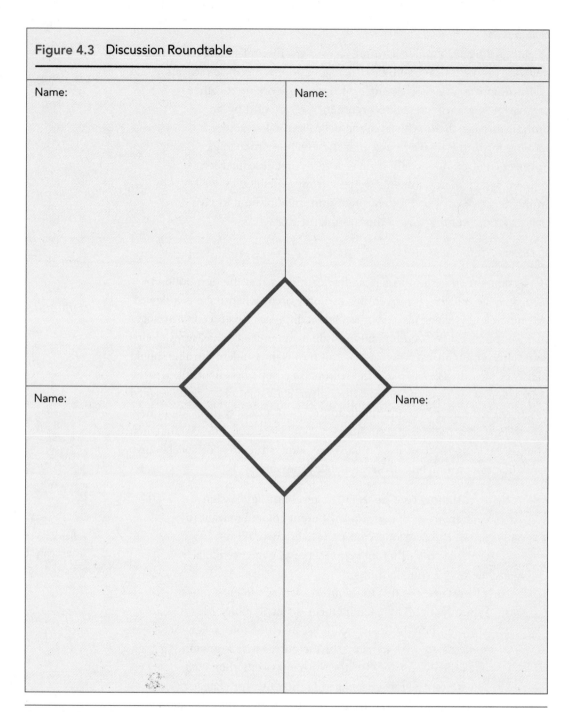

Figure 4.3   Discussion Roundtable

Name:

Name:

Name:

Name:

- **A discussion roundtable:** Another way to ensure group and individual accountability is through the use of a discussion roundtable. Students can simply fold a piece of paper like the one in Figure 4.3. As they read a selected piece of text, they take notes in the upper-left quadrant. They then take turns discussing the text and recording the content that their peers share in the other quadrants. At the end of the conversation they can summarize their understanding of the text, identify the theme, or ask questions (depending on the task assigned the teacher) in the area in the center.

Students need time every day, in every class, to practice their collaborative conversations.

Student self-assessments are also useful when developing collaborative learning skills in the classroom. Students in secondary school are developmentally more capable of distinguishing between the work of the group and their own role in influencing group dynamics. They can complete an individual feedback sheet that gives them an opportunity to reflect on their own contributions and set goals for future collaborative partnerships. These are completed and turned in with the written work. A combination of encouraging students' goal setting and providing them with opportunities for self-evaluation has been shown to improve academic achievement (Schunk, 1998). An example of an individual feedback sheet for older students appears in Figure 4.4. An individual self-assessment for younger students appears in Figure 4.5.

By establishing favorable conditions for collaborative learning, the peer-led portion of class time will run smoothly and result in rewarding exchanges among students. Keep in mind that these collaborative skills should be taught first, through modeling, and that students should then receive feedback about their performance in collaborative tasks. As students become more proficient in the curriculum and self-assessment, they will be prepared to apply them to collaborative learning situations.

When teachers use collaborative learning to help students meet the demands of accessing complex text, the most obvious implication it will have on their instruction will relate to the use of time. Students need time every day, in every class, to practice their collaborative conversations. That's not to say teachers should simply turn over their classrooms to students to talk, but rather that there should be expectations established for student-to-student interaction and that there should be an understanding that students will be held accountable for these interactions.

Figure 4.4 Individual Self-Assessment for Older Students

Name: _____ Date: _____

Name of Project/Assignment: _____

Evaluate your contributions to the collaborative task you completed. Read each statement and circle the number in the column on the right that represents *your* role best.

1 = never

2 = rarely

3 = sometimes

4 = usually

5 = always

I contributed ideas to the discussion.	1	2	3	4	5
I listened to the ideas of others.	1	2	3	4	5
I asked questions.	1	2	3	4	5
I located resources when needed.	1	2	3	4	5
I completed my tasks on time.	1	2	3	4	5
I did my fair share of the work.	1	2	3	4	5

My best contribution to this task was

The next time I work in a group, I will improve on

Based on my assessment, I would give myself a grade of _____.

Figure 4.5 Self-Assessment for Younger Students

Name: _____ Date: _____

Type of Work I Did: _____

Partners' Names: _____

How do I rate my work?

	Always	Sometimes	Not Yet
I asked questions.			
I listened when others talked.			
I did a fair share of the work.			
I used ideas from other people, not just my own.			
I was prepared to work.			

Video 4.8

Teacher
facilitates a
discussion
as practice
for students'
collaborative
work.

resources.corwin.com/
rigorousreadingfla

▶ Accessing Complex Texts Requires Student-to-Student Interaction

As we have noted, students must learn to interact with one another and the text if they are going to demonstrate proficiency with complex texts. There are a number of different ways to accomplish this, some of which have already been discussed, such as using literature circles and discussion roundtables. The remainder of this chapter provides a review of two additional collaborative learning structures that teachers can use to provide students opportunities to engage with their peers as they access complex texts: reciprocal teaching and collaborative strategic reading.

Reciprocal Teaching

As groups of students read and talk about what they read, they learn more. One structure for facilitating student reading and discussion is reciprocal teaching (Palincsar & Brown, 1984). During reciprocal teaching conversations, students assume practice with a specific comprehension strategy:

- Predicting
- Questioning
- Summarizing
- Clarifying

As they read, they pause periodically and talk about what they are reading. In some cases, they change roles each time they talk. In other cases, they practice the same role throughout the reading. It's important to note that reciprocal teaching groups do not have to consist of four students; **students can share a role, or a student can have more than one role.** The point of reciprocal teaching is to encourage reading, and deep understanding, of a piece of text. For example, during their discussion of immigration, as part of a unit on industrialization in America, students in Javier Vaca's U.S. history class engaged in reciprocal teaching when they encountered complex texts. Part of the conversation of one group highlights the learning that occurred:

Marco:	So, I have a question. What does it mean "push and pull"? What does that have to do with immigration?

Daisy: I think that they're saying that there were things that pushed the immigrants out of their home countries. Like, for example, some people weren't respected because of their religion.

Alexis: Yeah, and then some people were pushed out because they didn't have enough money. That was gonna be part of my summary, because they are saying that when people cannot afford to live in a place, they want to look for a new opportunity.

Uriel: That's the pull, right? Because the U.S. was a place where people could go to get a better life, and make enough money to take care of their family. So, I'll make a prediction. I predict that the next section will tell why that didn't work, because we still have a lot of poverty here, so it couldn't have all worked.

Vanessa: I remember that part where it said that the immigrants thought that "the streets were paved with gold." See, right here [pointing to a place in the text], but they weren't. They were just normal streets, but that was a pull, to think that the U.S. had so much money that they put gold on the street.

The point of reciprocal teaching is to encourage reading, and deep understanding, of a piece of text.

Collaborative Strategic Reading

Collaborative strategic reading (CSR) is a technique used by small groups of heterogeneously grouped students to read and comprehend text (Klinger & Vaughn, 1998). Typically used in groups of five, it is well suited for use with informational text, although it can be used in conjunction with narrative text as well. When using this technique, a text is divided into smaller sections so that the group stops from time to time to discuss what they know so far and what is confusing or unclear. The strength of this approach lies in the use of cooperative learning principles to practice sound comprehension strategies. The following four strategies, which are described in the sections that follow, are used by the group to understand the text:

- Preview
- Click and clunk
- Get the gist
- Wrap up

By creating prediction questions, students can begin to anticipate the information they may encounter during the reading.

Each of these strategies is taught and practiced in a whole-class context until students are able to use them without teacher support. A study of CSR in fourth-grade classrooms found that students who had been carefully taught each of the strategies focused the majority of their talk (65%) on the content of the reading, and another 25% on the procedural aspects of CSR; in contrast, only 2% of their talk was off task (Klinger, Vaughn, & Schumm, 1998).

Before the Reading: Preview

This step is performed before the reading. Students discuss what they already know about the topic of the reading and make predictions about what may be learned in the reading. By creating prediction questions, students can begin to anticipate the information they may encounter during the reading.

During the Reading: Click and Clunk

Click is the term used by the authors to describe smooth reading that makes sense to the student, much like the hum of a well-oiled machine. On the other hand, *clunk* describes the times when a reader encounters an unfamiliar word or concept. Together, clicks and clunks represent self-monitoring behaviors used by fluent readers. The clunks signal to the readers that other strategies for resolving comprehension problems are needed. After noticing that a problem has occurred, the reader can

- *reread* the sentence or paragraph;
- *read ahead* until the end of the sentence or paragraph;
- *analyze* the word for familiar affixes or root words; or
- *ask* his or her partner what it means.

During CSR, students read a passage from the text and then discuss their clunks. Using their collective knowledge, they clarify each other's understanding of the word or concept in question.

During the Reading: Get the Gist

At the end of each section of the passage, students summarize the main ideas and important facts. Like prediction and self-monitoring, summarizing is a comprehension behavior used by fluent readers (Brown & Day, 1983). Both click and clunk and get the gist are repeated several times until the entire reading has been completed.

After the Reading: Wrap Up

Once the group has finished with the reading, they revisit the predictions they made to check for accuracy. They also generate questions and answers that focus on the main ideas and important facts.

Students are initially assigned roles in CSR so that the discussion will flow more smoothly, and in time, these distinctions are faded as groups become more proficient with the process. These roles include the following:

- **Leader:** makes sure the strategies are used and seeks help from the teacher when needed
- **Clunk expert:** leads discussion on how to figure out unknown words or concepts
- **Announcer:** makes sure everyone has a chance to participate
- **Reporter:** shares the group's work during the "share" portion of the language arts workshop
- **Timer:** monitors the time so the group can complete the task during collaborative learning

Like prediction and self-monitoring, summarizing is a comprehension behavior used by fluent readers.

A group of third-grade students used CSR with the picture book *Stick Out Your Tongue!* (Bonsignore, 2001). An excerpt of the book read,

> Moths and butterflies use their tongues like straws to suck the sweet nectar from flowers.
>
> The tongue of an insect like a moth or butterfly is quite different from the tongues of other animals. These insects have a proboscis, a mouthpart that extends out and forms a long, thin tube much like a tiny straw. The moth or butterfly sticks the proboscis deep into the heart of the flower blossom and sucks the sweet nectar. One moth in Madagascar has a proboscis that is nine inches long! That's about as long as your mom's foot! (p. 3)

Ting, the leader of the group, asked everyone to read the page, then called on Kimberly, the clunk expert, to start the discussion about difficult vocabulary. "Did anyone have a clunk—a tricky word?"

Gaining access to complex text requires collaborative conversations because students need to talk about texts and make meaning with their peers.

"I had a bunch of them," said Marvin. Alicia, the announcer, reminded him to pick one so that everyone would have a turn. "I pick this word, then," said Marvin, pointing to *proboscis*. "I don't even know how to say it!"

Kimberly followed. "I had trouble with that one, too. Let's look at the list to see how we can figure it out. Let's reread the sentence." After all of them finished rereading, Marvin exclaimed, "There it is! It's 'a mouthpart that extends out and forms a long, thin tube.' It's right here in the picture." He points to the illustration of a moth using his proboscis to suck nectar from the center of a daisy. "The illustrator even drew a picture of a boy drinking from a straw to remind us of how it works," offered Wilfredo. The leader continued the conversation, and the group discussed *blossom* (Marvin knew this word), *nectar* (they made a connection to *nectarine* and decided it was something sweet), and *Madagascar* (they used context clues to determine that it was a place, then consulted an atlas to pinpoint its location).

Wilfredo, the timer, reminded the group that they needed to "get the gist" if they were going to finish this passage. After discussing the main idea of the passage, they each wrote the following sentence in their journal:

Moths and butterflies use a proboscis to suck nectar from flowers.

After reading three more pages of the book together, the group had developed several summary sentences, which they incorporated into their written summary of the book.

The following are some additional evidence-based speaking and listening instructional routines that have been useful for students:

- **Readers' theater**, in which students practice reading and rereading a script, either one that was prepared for them or one they developed collaboratively, based on an informational text they have studied (e.g., Young & Rasinski, 2009). Students are expected to present that text to the rest of the class while others listen. To ensure that they are listening, teachers often ask students to take notes, write down questions, or retell the information presented to a partner. For example, during their investigation of earth and the solar system, the fifth-grade students in Ms. Harris's class collaboratively read *Moon Power* (Evans, 2011) and then created a script to share with the rest of the class. The other students in the class selected their own texts, such as excerpts from *All About Space* (Becklake, 1998), and developed scripts to share.

- **Presentations,** in which students research a topic and then share their findings with their peers, either in small groups or in a large group (Fisher, McDonald, & Frey, 2013). Often, students are asked to provide their peers with feedback about their presentation skills. For example, the students in Mr. Ramirez's sixth-grade class examined the impact of trash, with a focus on space junk and the garbage patch in the Pacific Ocean. As part of their investigation, they read *Plastic Ahoy!* (Newman, 2014), and each group was asked to present on one chapter of the book. One group focused on ocean currents and the creation of the Pacific garbage patch, using a Prezi with Google Earth images and narration.

- **Listening stations,** in which students listen to digital recordings of their teacher reading a complex informational text aloud and then discuss the questions the teacher poses at the end of the recording (Skouge, Rao, & Boisvert, 2007). These readings include instructions for students (e.g., Put your finger on the title. Check your partner; does he or she have the title identified correctly?) as well as explanations of difficult words and concepts (e.g., The word *stabilizing* means to hold still. So the author is saying that the Slinky was invented to hold ships more still so that they wouldn't rock so much).

Technology offers teachers new ways to engage students in speaking and listening tasks. Even very young children are learning to follow oral directions while using tablets. The following are some of the enhancing speaking and listening tasks that can be used in elementary content area instruction:

- **Listening gallery walk,** in which students create a visual image, record themselves talking about the image, and then code it with a symbol that will allow others to access the digital file. One way to do this is with QR codes that can be printed and included in the image itself. Alternatively, students can use the Aurasma app. This is an augmented reality application that allows users to create and post video to enhance a viewing experience. For example, some museums use Aurasma for their patrons to view additional content whenever they point a smartphone or tablet at a display. In terms of classroom application, students can create their own videos and pair them with displayed work. For example, during their investigation of artists, students in Ms. Bledsoe's third-grade class narrated their original artwork that had been inspired by a specific artist. When a tablet enabled with Aurasma was pointed at one of the art pieces, the video that accompanied the art played. When parents visited for open house, they were able to see their children talking about their work and to learn more about the other students in the class.

- **Photo narratives,** in which students collect images and then record a narrative to accompany the images. For example, the first graders in Mr. Munoz's classroom planted seeds. Each day, they took a picture of the container in which their seed was planted. Mr. Munoz read aloud the text *From Seed to Plant* (Gibbons, 1993) several times as the plants grew. He helped his students create a time-lapse video using QuickTime with the images, and the students recorded their narrative about the growth of the plant that accompanied the video.
- **Digital storytelling,** in which students create original narrative and informational pieces. The Storybird app allows you to access thousands of illustrations and photographs to illustrate original pieces of writing. These are best when completed collaboratively to create lots of opportunities for students to engage in meaningful discussion with one another. The VoiceThread website offers two-way communication between writers and readers. Like with Storybird,

students create a digital story using the VoiceThread tools and their own illustrations. In addition, they dictate the text for each page. Subsequent listeners can either listen to the writer's own voice or read the dictated script. Importantly, readers can then pose questions and offer connections that are, in turn, viewed by other readers. As part of their social studies curriculum, Ms. Thompson's second-grade students used VoiceThread to develop a class digital book on people who make a difference in their community. Ms. Thompson compiled each student's contribution and uploaded them to the VoiceThread website. Later, in the centers, students viewed the class book and recorded their comments and questions. Ms. Thompson then had the entire class view the completed digital story, with their questions included, so the class could continue the conversation about the topic.

▶ Summary

Gaining access to complex text requires collaborative conversations because students need to talk about texts and make meaning with their peers. In previous chapters, we explained how modeling academic discourse is a vital first step in fostering critical thinking. Students then begin to apply this discourse under the watchful eye of the teacher during close reading and scaffolded reading. But without opportunities to use this on their own during collaborative learning, students don't get the chance to practice how they "talk" to themselves as they read complex text independently. Collaborative learning, whether through literature circles, discussion roundtables, reciprocal teaching, or collaborative strategic reading, gives students the time they need to witness their own thinking and learn about the ideas of others.

iStock.com/Sneksy

Access Point Four

An Independent Reading Staircase

Although it is independent reading time in Mrs. Garcia's fourth-grade class, it is far from silent. Several children are clustered in a comfortable corner of the room where rocking chairs and braided rugs offer an inviting space to get lost in a book. Others students are reading at their tables on iPads. Trisha and Leon are looking through a basket in the classroom library labeled *Migration and Immigration*, while Kaleem, Sonje, and Melissa are already reading. The pages of their books sprout sticky notes with handwritten annotations.

While most of the students are settling into their independent reading, Mrs. Garcia is seated at a small table in another corner of the room. To her left are a binder for her student reading conference notes and a stack of observation forms like the one in Figure 5.1. Patrice, a girl with braids and a quick smile, is discussing her book with her teacher.

"Tell me about the book you're reading, Patrice. What has happened so far?" asks Mrs. Garcia.

Figure 5.1   Reading Conference Form

Name: _____   Date: _____

Title and Author: _____

Retelling (check all that apply)

❑ discusses important events

❑ offers salient details

❑ uses evidence from the text to support retelling

❑ states opinion

❑ provides textual support for opinion

❑ needs prompts to expand answers

Notes:

Oral Reading Fluency

❑ reads accurately

❑ fluently, in long phrases

❑ choppy, in short phrases

❑ word by word

❑ with expression

❑ flat and without expression

Notes:

Goals for Next Meeting:

"It's really good!" offers Patrice.

> I'm reading *Seeds of Hope* [Gregory, 2001], and it's about
> a girl named Susanna who is traveling on a ship to get
> to Oregon. Her mom died on the ship, and her dad lost
> all their money. Now they're going to go to California
> because they heard about gold.

This novel, told in diary form, has been a popular choice among many of the students in the class during the last few weeks.

After asking a few more questions to confirm Patrice's comprehension, Mrs. Garcia asks her to read a passage that was meaningful to her. Patrice chooses the journal entry when Susanna's father tells her they will be going to California instead of Oregon. While Patrice reads, Mrs. Garcia makes notes about Patrice's reading fluency and her use of expression. Mrs. Garcia then asks Patrice about observations she has made during the reading. Patrice turns to the section of the book about when Susanna's father tells her he is going to be a gold miner, not a doctor.

> I was thinking about another book I read this year called
> *Riding Freedom* [Ryan, 1999]. Susanna reminds me of
> Charley in *Riding Freedom* because she has to learn how
> to rely on herself when her parents aren't there for her
> anymore.

A guiding principle of the Florida English Language Arts Standards is that students should achieve a level of independence that makes it possible for them to express their own thoughts and ideas and to understand the thoughts and ideas of others.

As their reading conference draws to an end, Mrs. Garcia and Patrice develop a goal for Patrice to look for historical connections since they are studying the California Gold Rush in social studies. With that, Patrice leaves the table with her book in hand. Looking back over her shoulder, Patrice remarks, "I'll let you know what happens next!"

A guiding principle of the Florida English Language Arts Standards is that students should achieve a level of independence that makes it possible for them to express their own thoughts and ideas and to understand the thoughts and ideas of others. In part, access to complex texts comes from engaging in deliberate and sustained practice in reading. Marie Clay (2001) refers to this as "the high demand from the first days of school for children to read and write texts according to their competencies but always as independently as possible" (p. 48). After all, as educators, our intent is to develop a set of skills in each learner that ultimately can be used outside the presence of the teacher. Like all aspects of learning, each student's ability to engage in independent tasks is fostered through explicit instruction.

An important advantage of developing independent learners is that the teacher can then use his or her time to support the efforts of individual students.

An important advantage of developing independent learners is that the teacher can then use his or her time to support the efforts of individual students. Within every class, there exist some students who need more specialized teacher supports; as well, every student, regardless of achievement level, needs personal contact with the teacher. As busy classroom teachers know, this can happen on a consistent basis only when all the students know how to work collaboratively and independently. A powerful practice for making contact with each student is known as *conferring*. Teachers confer with students through rich conversations about their reading practices.

This chapter focuses on the roles of students and teachers as they access complex texts during independent learning. While students work independently to apply the literacy skills and strategies they have been taught during modeling, close reading, scaffolded reading instruction, and collaborative learning, teachers are conferring with students individually to engage them in important conversations about their learning.

▶ The Goals of Independent Learning

Video 5.1

Doug discusses independent learning.

resources.corwin.com/ rigorousreadingfla

It seems as if the practice of having students working quietly and independently on individual tasks is as old a concept as school itself. Many of us have memories of toiling away on worksheets while the teacher walked up and down the aisles. Rarely were any words exchanged, other than those pertaining to simple questions about the assignment at hand. When completed, these worksheets were turned in to be graded. Rarely did we understand how any of these worksheets connected to our learning. The goal instead seemed to be to complete the workbook or the pile of dittos in our folders.

There are several drawbacks associated with this approach to independent work. For one, the work completed independently may focus on many repetitions of the same isolated skills, leading to disengagement and boredom. This is especially true for struggling readers who will sometimes focus on getting the assignment done rather than on the intended learning outcomes that were built into the lesson design (Anderson, Brubaker, Alleman-Brooks, & Duffy, 1985). For example, envision the student who completes a spelling assignment of writing each word 10 times by instead writing each letter in a vertical column of 10 until the entire word is completed. After completing the list, the student is no closer to remembering how to spell the word than when she began. When we talk about independent learning, we are not referring to activities like worksheets intended to keep students quiet and occupied. The goal of independent learning is to empower students to develop self-regulation skills, increase their sense of competence, and set goals for themselves. Below, we discuss these three goals in greater detail.

Self-Regulation

Independent learning provides students with opportunities to self-regulate—to manage their time, monitor their progress, and solve problems. In their study of third graders, Stright and Supplee (2002) found that students were more likely to ask for help and monitor their progress during independent learning when they had been taught how to do so. Good and Brophy (2003) consider self-regulation to be an essential component of the curriculum:

> Students cannot learn self-regulation and self-control if the teacher does all of the alerting, accountability, and so on. They need to be taught to manage time (we have fifteen minutes to finish a task) and to define their own work and procedures (what is the critical problem—how else might the problem be approached?). This appropriate management necessitates that rules and structures—the scaffolding—be progressively altered to encourage more responsibility for self-control. (p. 137)

A powerful practice for making contact with each student is known as conferring. Teachers confer with students through rich conversations about their reading practices.

When students have daily opportunities to engage in meaningful independent learning, they not only apply literacy skills and strategies but also develop the ability to regulate and monitor their pace of work and hone their problem-solving skills.

Competence

In addition to helping students self-regulate, independent learning provides them with a chance to develop a sense of competence. The concept of competence hinges on a learner's perception of her abilities and on her understanding of the effort needed to accomplish a task. While many speak of the importance of self-esteem in the learning process, it is *competence* that really contributes to a learner's self-esteem. It is through a sense of competence that self-esteem is built. This, in turn, increases motivation, because we are motivated to do those things we know we do well. When students have the opportunity to explore and experience their own competence through independent learning, their self-efficacy improves, and they begin to believe that learning is under their control (Yeager & Dweck, 2012).

When we talk about independent learning, we are not referring to activities like worksheets intended to keep students quiet and occupied.

Goal Setting

A final positive aspect of independent learning is that it allows students to gain experience at setting and achieving goals. Alexander and Jetton (2000, p. 297) describe students as possessing one or more of the following goal orientations that serve to propel or inhibit their learning.

- **Performance goals:** Students who view learning through this lens are interested in teacher recognition and good grades. The extrinsic rewards of the task become the goal for completing the work.
- **Mastery goals:** Students with this orientation are interested in the content of the task and the opportunity to expand their own knowledge base.
- **Work-avoidant goals:** Some students are primarily interested in completing the task with the least amount of effort necessary.

All students are motivated by a combination of these goals to varying degrees. However, it is important to recognize that all of these orientations exist and that the second category—that of the mastery goals—is the one that teachers should aim to cultivate. Independent learning provides teachers with the perfect opportunity to make this happen, as this is a format in which students will experience many opportunities to set their own goals and monitor their progress toward attaining them. In addition, the practice of independent learning provides teachers with opportunities to monitor their students—through conferring—throughout the learning process.

▶ Accessing Complex Texts Requires Wide, Independent Reading

One way to ensure that students read in class is to provide them with time to read. Unlike silent sustained reading in which students read texts of their own choosing, independent reading constrains students' choices, and they read increasingly complex texts. For example, earth science teacher Adam Renick provides 10 minutes each day for his students to independently read complex texts about the content they are studying. Mr. Renick notes, "Scientists read every day as part of their job, and I want my students to have that same experience." Reading widely builds background knowledge and vocabulary, which is essential for strengthening disciplinary knowledge. Students can't draw on personal experiences alone when learning about the physical, social, and biological world, particularly as the content grows more technical in middle school. They must read complex texts that develop their knowledge. There is evidence that when students are provided with time for independent reading of content-area-aligned texts, their academic performance improves (Fisher, Ross, & Grant, 2010).

Students were more likely to ask for help and monitor their progress during independent learning when they had been taught how to do so.

To understand complex texts, students must master content-area knowledge. They should view reading as a means of gaining such knowledge. Stated a different way, knowledge cannot be built simply by telling students what they need to know. They need to see texts as an important source of information. Thoughtfully chosen independent reading materials afford students with opportunities to (1) apply what they have been taught about comprehension and (2) build their knowledge about the topics they are studying. It's really like climbing a staircase. It takes you to a new level, but that doesn't mean that you have to always be at that level. The staircase represents an effort but a goal that can be accomplished.

This staircase has to be built over years, as well as over units of study and phases of instruction. The texts selected for independent reading on a given day should be complex, but perhaps not as complex as those used during close reading or scaffolded reading that occurs on the same day. However, there should be a steady, forward progression in the complexity of texts used in independent reading and collaborative conversations; this progression should mirror the trajectory of increasing text complexity followed when engaging in close readings.

Independent reading is important because students need time to try on the strategies they have been learning. Thus, the practice of independent reading is connected with the modeling and scaffolded instruction students have received. The effectiveness of independent reading is rooted in two concepts: increasing reading volume and developing positive reading attitudes.

When students have the opportunity to explore and experience their own competence through independent learning, their self-efficacy improves, and they begin to believe that learning is under their control.

Reading Volume

Reading volume is a measure of the amount of reading a learner engages in both in school and at home. Stanovich (1986) examined the relationship between students' volume of outside reading and their ability to read. This study confirmed what many teachers had always known—the more reading students do, the better their reading becomes. A related study compared students' standardized test scores in reading and the amount of outside reading they did. As in the earlier study, the results indicated that there was a strong correlation between reading volume and achievement (Anderson, Wilson, & Fielding, 1988). A table of the results can be seen in Figure 5.2. These and similar studies spurred educators' interest in carving out a portion of the school day during which students could read independently for an extended period of time.

Positive Reading Attitudes

In addition to exploring the connection between reading and achievement, studies have demonstrated the importance of positive reading attitudes. Concern over this topic is well founded because positive student attitudes toward reading decline during the late elementary years, especially among boys (Kush & Watkins, 1996). A large-scale study based on national testing results suggested that students who had positive attitudes toward reading (described as *engaged readers*) outperformed older, disengaged readers (Campbell, Voekl, & Donahue, 1997). An analysis of fourth graders' results on the same test revealed that engaged readers from low-income backgrounds outperformed disengaged readers from

Figure 5.2 Relationship Between Achievement and Independent Reading

Percentile Rank	Minutes of Reading per Day (Books)	Words Read per Year
98	65.0	4,358,000
90	21.1	1,823,000
80	14.2	1,146,000
70	9.6	622,000
60	6.5	432,000
50	4.6	282,000
40	3.2	200,000
30	1.8	106,000
20	0.7	21,000
10	0.1	8,000
2	0.0	0

Source: Adapted from Anderson et al. (1988). Used with permission.

higher socioeconomic backgrounds (Guthrie, Schafer, & Huang, 2001). These positive attitudes toward reading are developed through

- clear learning goals;
- texts that relate to a student's personal experiences;
- support from the teacher on making choices;
- texts with interesting topics;
- instruction in reading strategies;
- opportunities to collaborate with other students;
- a positive environment that is not driven by extrinsic rewards;

- evaluation that provides feedback on progress, rather than tests of knowledge;
- personal connections to the teacher; and
- cohesive instruction. (Guthrie & Wigfield, 2000)

Video 5.2

Student discusses SSR.
resources.corwin.com/ rigorousreadingfla

Differences Between SSR and Independent Reading

There are some differences between sustained silent reading (SSR) and independent reading, although both of them have their place in the classroom. In particular, they differ in terms of overall purpose, book selection and access, accountability, and roles of the student and teacher. A summary of these differences can be seen in Figure 5.3.

Goals and Purpose. The primary goal of SSR is to develop positive student attitudes toward reading and to encourage students to view reading as a recreational activity. On the other hand, the goal of independent reading is to provide time for practice of skills and strategies taught in other phases of instruction.

Book Selection. In SSR, the student makes the ultimate decision about what he or she will read. The teacher provides guidance and information about choosing books that are a "good fit," but a student is never discouraged from reading a particular book. In independent reading, the teacher has more influence over what will be read because the text should connect to the content being taught. In addition, the independent reading text should build the reading prowess of students, taking them up another step on their staircase to accessing complex texts.

Book Access. During independent reading, a narrow range of texts are made available because the purpose is to practice using a skill or strategy. In SSR, students have access to and read a wide range of materials, including nontraditional texts like comic books, magazines, and web-based information.

Accountability. During independent reading, students spend some of their time completing reviews, graphic organizers, précis writing, and written reflections about the reading. In SSR, nonaccountability is the hallmark. Students simply read.

Figure 5.3 Differences Between SSR and Independent Reading

	Sustained Silent Reading	Independent Reading
Goals and purpose	Reading for pleasure	Building mastery through practice
Book selection	Student choice with a wide range of genres and levels	Constrained choice of increasingly complex texts
Accountability	No records kept	Tasks and reflections are essential
What are students doing?	Reading quietly	Reading and writing reflections Conferring with teacher
What is the teacher doing?	Brief book talk Reading quietly	Conferring with students Observing Assessing
Follow-up activity	Students can volunteer to briefly talk about a book; this is not always a part of an SSR session.	Students discuss their reading. The discussion is related to the purpose set at the beginning of the session.

Student's Role. During SSR, students read until the end of the time allotted, then transition to the next activity. During independent reading, students may be reading, writing about their reading, or conferring with the teacher about their reading.

Teacher's Role. During SSR, the teacher reads to provide an adult model of recreational reading. During independent reading, the teacher is conferring with students, assessing and observing while students read.

Follow-Up Activities. In SSR, students may be invited to share a book they are reading. However, this is never a requirement, and students are free to volunteer or not. In independent reading, a sharing phase is included at the end of each reading period. The discussions students engage in during this sharing phase are based on the assignment that was given to them before the independent reading began.

One of the goals of independent reading is to provide students with an opportunity to write about thoughts, ideas, and evidence that connect to their reading.

Students Respond During Independent Reading

One of the goals of independent reading is to provide students with an opportunity to write about thoughts, ideas, and evidence that connect to their reading. These written responses are usually brief in nature, and teachers can use a variety of tools with their students to help them organize their thoughts as they are writing.

Comment Cards

Students use these simple note taking frameworks to jot down thoughts and ideas related to the strategies and skills they are practicing or the content they are learning. This is an early form of annotation for students who are just beginning to learn this skill. A sample comment card appears in Figure 5.4.

For example, Aida Allen asked her fifth graders to look for evidence of foreshadowing during independent reading. Jeremy reviewed the previous chapters he had already read and wrote several notes on his comment card about *Frindle* (Clements, 1996; see Figure 5.5).

Sticky Notes

As students become more adept at making notes as they are reading—and if they are not allowed to annotate directly on the text—they can move from comment cards to sticky notes. These small notes can be positioned to "underline" important passages students encounter. A challenge of using sticky notes is teaching students how to use them with an economy of words. Learners who have been accustomed to writing on 8-1/2″ × 11″ sheets of paper may attempt to crowd too many words onto these small notes. It is useful for them to have a bank of simple annotations available to help them abbreviate their thoughts while still preserving meaning.

Video 5.3

Teachers talk about the use of independent reading.
resources.corwin.com/ rigorousreadingfla

Figure 5.4 Comment Cards

Comment Card	Comment Card	Comment Card
During today's reading, I am looking for:	During today's reading, I am looking for:	During today's reading, I am looking for:
I found examples on:	*I found examples on:*	*I found examples on:*
Pg. _____	Pg. _____	Pg. _____
Pg. _____	Pg. _____	Pg. _____
Pg. _____	Pg. _____	Pg. _____
Pg. _____	Pg. _____	Pg. _____

Figure 5.5 Jeremy's Comment Card

Comment Card

During today's reading, I am looking for:

foreshadowing

I found examples on:

Pg. _1_____

Was Nick a troublemaker? Hard to say.

Pg. _8_____

Mrs. Granger didn't just enjoy the dictionary. She <u>loved</u> the dictionary—almost worshipped it.

Pg. _12_____

It was still a week before school and Nick already felt like fifth grade was going to be a very long year.

Pg. _____

Reflection Journals

Independent readers not only read for meaning; they also need to reflect on and discuss their readings with others. To support their discussions, students need to make notes and write down their thoughts and observations. The purpose for reading should be established at the beginning of the independent reading time, with appropriate instruction about what to look for in the reading. Many teachers find that instructing students to begin notes from each reading session on a new page of a reflection journal (complete with date, title, and relevant page numbers) is helpful for keeping students organized. These response journal entries can address a range of topics, but generally offer students the opportunities to engage in a meaningful transaction with the text. Students can then draw from the content of these reflection journals during class discussions to provide evidence from the texts they are reading; these journals are also read by the teacher.

There is a transaction that occurs between the text and the reader that makes each text–reader relationship unique.

Readers make meaning at the word level through understanding the vocabulary, and at the sentence and paragraph levels through understanding how ideas are crafted by the author to tell a story or forward a position on a topic. But readers also make meaning through their own transactions with the text. They activate their background knowledge to determine the veracity of the text—"Could this happen?" Finally, they analyze the text for its usefulness to them—"What did I learn from this text?" In other words, the words on the page do not simply lie there waiting to be consumed without analysis by the reader. Instead, there is a transaction that occurs between the text and the reader that makes each text–reader relationship unique. This is why, for example, one person can love a book while another considers it a complete waste of time.

Those transactions form the basis for reader response theory (Rosenblatt, 1938/1995). Reader response theory suggests that all reading experiences can be described as a balance between efferent (information-seeking) and aesthetic (emotional) responses. It is important to note that one is not more valued than another, but rather that each reading experience can be represented on a continuum between these two response types. For example, a reader's response to Robert Frost's poem "Stopping by Woods on a Snowy Evening" may be primarily aesthetic as the reader enjoys how Frost crafts his words and meter. However, there is still likely to be an efferent component as the reader constructs his understanding of the woods. At the other extreme, a reader's response to the book *How Animals Shed Their Skin* (Tatham, 2002) may be primarily efferent as he or she looks for information about leopard frogs. Even then, there is likely to be an aesthetic response as well when they view the weird and wonderful animals in the photographs. Although it is not necessary to teach students these terms (we shudder at the thought of a second grader offering, "I would like to make an aesthetic response to *Madeline*"), it is important that they have many opportunities to explore their transactions with the texts they are reading. As they gain insight into the way they are interacting with the texts, they will become conscious of their learning and build their metacognitive skills. In addition, this awareness will also feed into their ability to understand their levels of comprehension and self-monitor accordingly.

It should never be assumed that students know how to participate in rich discussions about a text. These skills should be explicitly taught so that students can begin to fully participate in this academic discourse.

Students Talk About Texts

One of the desired outcomes of independent reading is that students will talk about the texts they are reading in collaborative conversations. These conversations can take place in small-group collaborative sessions or in a whole-class format. Providing students with time to share offers numerous benefits for readers. First, it is useful for oral language development at both the social and content levels. For English language learners in particular, it is an occasion to engage in academic language. Book discussions also provide opportunities for students to hone listening skills, particularly when they are encouraged to make connections to peers' comments rather than to direct their conversations to the teacher. These collaborative conversations are critical for helping students clarify their understanding of a text, ask questions, and deepen their understanding of complex texts. As with all aspects of instruction, it should never be assumed that students know how to participate in rich discussions about a text. Therefore, these skills should be explicitly taught so that students can begin to fully participate in this academic discourse.

An example of a collaborative conversation follows:

It is early October, and the students in Lisa Targas's first-grade classroom have been reading sequence stories to understand how an author can tell a tale that builds on the action. During her modeling, Ms. Targas used *Joseph Had a Little Overcoat* (Tayback, 1999) to chart the sequence of events that occurred as Joseph's coat became more worn and was converted into a jacket, vest, tie, patch, and button. During collaborative reading, students worked in small groups to create similar charts for *There Was an Old Lady Who Swallowed a Fly* (Tayback, 2007).

After multiple experiences with sequence texts, students were ready to read and discuss others during independent reading. Ms. Targas created a box full of books with stories that use sequence as a major feature. Students selected titles and created their own sequence charts, using a format similar to the one seen in Figure 5.6. While all of the students worked, Ms. Targas met with select individual students to confer about their work and also offered support for others who needed clarification on their reading.

When students finished reading and responding, they began to discuss the books they had chosen. Ms. Targas prompted,

When students become more motivated to read, as is likely to occur when they are reading on a regular basis, it's more likely that they'll read at home.

> Remember to use your journals because that's where you have some of your good ideas written down. We're going to start by talking about the books you read. We paid attention to the sequences in our stories today so let's start there. Who would like to begin?

The class discussed the plots of the stories and the sequences used. Stephanie remarked that her book, *The Napping House* (Wood, 2009), reminded her of the time the ceiling fan fell down in the living room one night and woke everyone in the house. As the students discussed the content, Ms. Targas made notes about students' performance. These notes serve as fodder for future instruction, including the individual conferences that she will have with her students.

▶ Increasing At-Home Reading

In addition to the independent reading time teachers provide students during the school day, to meet the standards and ensure that all students achieve at high levels, they have to engage in distributed practice outside of school. The correlational data about reading volume and achievement we presented earlier in this chapter was based on reading that students did outside of school. When students become more motivated to read, as is likely to occur when they are reading on a regular basis, it's more likely

Figure 5.6 Reading Journal Format for Sequence Stories

Title of book: _____ Author: _____

This book was about

The best part of this book was

One way the author could change this book is

Here's what happened in the text (use pictures and words)

1	2	3
4	5	6

that they'll read at home. There are a few things that teachers can do to encourage students to increase their at-home reading volume, and one of them we have already discussed, which is to provide students opportunities to talk about what they are reading during school. In addition to these very valuable discussions about texts, the following three actions can help:

Access. If there is little to read in your house, you're less likely to read. To raise the volume of reading outside the school day, students must have access to texts. There have been a number of efforts to "flood" students with things to read (e.g., Elley, 2000) to address the need for students to have access to reading materials. The International Literacy Association (ILA) recommends a minimum of seven books per student in the class. That would mean that a classroom library for a group of 28 students would need nearly 200 texts for students to read. In addition to classroom libraries, school libraries can be additional resources that provide students with access to texts. ILA (2000) recommends a ratio of 20 books per child for school libraries.

However, Newman's (2017) study of 15 childcare centers in an urban area serving 501 children demonstrated that there was little impact from a book flood alone, noting, "the results of our study suggest that access to such books may be necessary, but it was clearly insufficient to enhance early literacy skills" (p. 18).

Choice. When students have choice over their reading materials, they are more likely to read. Choice is key to motivation and academic independence (Schunk, Meece, & Pintrich, 2013). Teachers can assign reading for students to do, especially during class time, when scaffolding can be provided. But to increase reading volume, teachers have to expand the amount of choice students have in what they read. Students who have opportunities to choose their own books develop elaborate strategies for selecting books and are more likely to become intrinsically motivated readers. In their studies of reading motivation, Guthrie et al. (2007) noted, "students expressed that they like both making their own book choices, as well as having close, trusted others choose books for them" (p. 306). Choice does not necessarily mean "read whatever you want," but it might. For example, students could be provided a choice of texts based on a theme or essential question under investigation. Or students could be invited to continue reading their independent-reading text. Or students might be offered free range to read what they want.

Book Talks and "Blessing Books." When trusted others make recommendations about a text, potential readers are more likely to read it. To promote wide reading outside the school day, students need recommendations from others. Book talks conducted by trusted adults and peers can spur voluntary reading. Gambrell calls this "blessed books" (Marinak & Gambrell, 2016) and suggests that teachers talk about several books that readers in the class might enjoy. These books are then placed on a special shelf, face forward if possible, for students to select. Wozniak (2011) conducted an intervention to increase voluntary reading among sixth graders in her school using book talks to anchor the program. Teachers spent 10 minutes three times a week introducing books to their students. Students were also provided with 15 to 20 minutes of unrestricted reading time with any book in the classroom, including short partner discussions. In this investigation, "There were no guidelines, so their discussions took on different forms" such as discussing what was happening in the book or making recommendations (p. 20). Students were free to talk about their reading rather than be restricted by school-bound book reports that are dutifully delivered but rarely deeply felt (White & Greenfield, 1995). The results of the intervention included positive changes in measures of reading attitude, self-efficacy, and reading outside of school.

The purpose of a reading conference is determined by the teacher and student together because the conversation should be a give-and-take of questions and ideas.

Students can "bless" books, too. As Hudson (2016) notes, primary students can conduct peer-led book talks, promoting interest while also learning about one another as readers. Hudson modeled book talks herself, introducing a few titles each day, and included some specifics about the title, name of the author, and a brief description of characters and plot. Most importantly, she added recommendations. Within a short time, her first-grade students were leading book talks each week on a rotating basis.

▶ Accessing Complex Texts Requires Conferring

When students are reading or writing independently, the teacher can use some of this time to meet individually with students. Conferring provides the teacher with an excellent assessment opportunity. These conferences allow the teacher to gauge the progress of each student, clarify information, and provide feedback for next steps. In addition, teachers keep records of these conversations for later reflection about individual student progress. These conferences are brief in nature (a few minutes or so) and can be used as a follow up to inform further scaffolded instruction. Teachers usually average between three and five student conferences per independent reading session.

Effective conferences include four elements. Because each conference event is short, these elements come into play very quickly. When conferring, the student and teacher use the learner's work as evidence. The teacher focuses on only one or two points during a single session. A helpful sequence for a conference is as follows:

- **Inquiry:** The teacher begins by conversing with the student about his or her work. The goal is to assess the student on one literacy focus topic per session.
- **Decisions:** Based on the evidence culled from the opening conversation, the teacher rapidly makes a decision about what should be taught next.
- **Instruction:** The teacher provides a minute or two of procedural, literary, or strategic instruction to help the student move to the next level of independent learning, and the student attempts the work with teacher support.
- **Recordkeeping:** The teacher makes anecdotal notes about the main points of the conference.

The notes generated from these conferences will be consulted again later for further instructional and evaluative decisions. It is not uncommon for teachers to customize their conferring forms to meet the unique needs of their classrooms. However, a basic format for a conference appears in Figure 5.7.

The goal of a reading conference is to engage a student in a conversation about the book he or she is reading. The purpose of a reading conference is determined by the teacher and student together because the conversation should be a give-and-take of questions and ideas. In any case, the student and teacher should use both the text and reading journal during the conversation. The scenario at the beginning of this chapter is a reading conference. Useful goals for a reading conference include the following:

- Discuss something in the text.
- Ask about areas of confusion.

Video 5.4

Asking children to use textual evidence in kindergarten.
resources.corwin.com/ rigorousreadingfla

Figure 5.7 Overview Form for Conferences

Name	Date	Type of Conference	Topic Discussed	Next Meeting	Goal for Next Meeting

Types of conferences:
RC: reading conference
WC: writing conference
O: other (specify)

- Discuss the author's purpose or craft.
- Review the student's list of books read.
- Set reading goals together.

▶ Summary

Independent reading is a time when students get to practice applying what they have been learning during other parts of the instructional day. Typically, students read a book that has been selected by the teacher because it features opportunities for them to use or draw from techniques or content they have already been learning. Students may respond in a reading journal and then use these notes to participate in discussions with other students. Teachers and students confer about independent reading and writing. The goal of these conferences is to engage students in an individual conversation about their work. A useful sequence for teachers to use during a conference is to first inquire, then make decisions about the immediate needs of the student. Teachers should be sure to note important details of the conference for next time and to end the session with a goal that the student can accomplish. When students read independently and confer with their teachers about the texts they are reading, they begin to access complex texts in new ways, ways that build the habits necessary for them to read for meaning in college and throughout their careers.

When students read independently and confer with their teachers about the texts they are reading, they begin to access complex texts in new ways.

iStock.com/recep-bg

Access Point Five

Assessing Students' Understanding

Internet searches often yield surprising results. Recently, Nancy searched one of her favorite sayings in preparation for a presentation she was doing about assessments: "You can't fatten sheep by weighing them." One of the results was an article from the April 1908 issue of the *Farm Journal* on early spring lambs. Among the advice to sheep farmers? Take care in apportioning their rations so as not to overfeed, provide healthy living conditions so they can grow, take careful measure of their progress, and keep this piece of wisdom in mind: "Study your sheep and know them not only as a flock but separately, and remember that they have an individuality as surely as your horse or cow" (Brick, 1908, p. 154).

Students are not sheep, of course, but our role as cultivators of young people has much in common with the role of a livestock farmer.

Without ways to look for patterns across students, formative assessments become a frustrating academic exercise.

As educators, we recognize the importance of a healthy learning climate, and we seek to create one each day. In addition, we apportion information so that students can act on their growing knowledge of the discipline. And we measure their progress throughout to see whether they are making expected gains. As part of effective practice, teachers routinely check for understanding through the learning process. This is most commonly accomplished by asking questions, analyzing tasks, and administering low-stakes quizzes to measure the extent to which students are acquiring new information and skills. But it's one thing to gather information (we're good at that); it's another to respond in meaningful ways and then plan for subsequent instruction. Without processes to provide students with solid feedback that yields deeper understanding, checking for understanding devolves into a game of "guess what's in the teacher's brain." And without ways to look for patterns across students, formative assessments become a frustrating academic exercise. Knowing both the flock and the individuals in it are the essential pieces of the puzzle for those in the cultivation business.

Video 6.1

Teacher reflects on her close reading instruction.
resources.corwin.com/ rigorousreadingfla

▶ Checking for Understanding

Before students can receive feedback, their peers or teachers need to know what they understood and did not understand. As we will discuss later, making instructional decisions based on student performance requires the collection of evidence. There are many ways to check for understanding that can guide the feedback students receive from peers or teachers. We see checking for understanding as a critical step in providing students access to complex texts, because analyzing the data can reveal areas of mastery and areas of confusion, allowing the teacher to take action.

"Did everybody get that?" says Mr. Unger. Rafael, a student in the class, thinks to himself, *No, I have no idea what you're talking about, but I'm not about to let everyone know that I'm confused.* And so the game continues, with the teacher thinking he is checking for understanding and accepting the silence as an indicator that learning has occurred. In reality, despite quality instruction, Mr. Unger has no idea whether learning has or has not taken place.

How then could Mr. Unger check for understanding? What does quality checking for understanding look and sound like? Our analysis of classroom instruction and assessment suggests that there are several ways teachers can check for understanding, including the use of oral language, questioning, writing, projects and performances, and tests (Fisher & Frey, 2014). When teachers use these procedures, they know which students understand the content and which students need additional instruction. Checking for understanding, then, is an important part of a formative assessment system. Looking at student responses or student work informs the teacher, and that information can be acted upon to create better understanding. Importantly, checking for understanding has to occur throughout the lesson, at least every 5 to 10 minutes, if teachers want to maintain the rigor of the lesson while supporting student learning. Let's consider some of the common ways that teachers can check for understanding.

Video 6.2

Teacher promotes students' reflection and metacognition after lesson.
resources.corwin.com/ rigorousreadingfla

Oral Language

One effective way to check for understanding is through oral language: speaking and listening. When students are doing the talking, the teacher has a chance to assess understanding. There are a number of classroom structures that provide students an opportunity to talk, including think–pair–share, reciprocal teaching, literacy circles, discussion prompts, and Socratic seminars. For example, as Ms. Ramirez listens to her students discussing a book they are reading as part of their book club, she notices that they are not justifying their responses with evidence from the text. They are skilled at summarizing, but the lack of evidence in their discussions indicates a need to devote additional instructional time to this practice.

In addition to listening as students interact, retellings are a valuable way to check for understanding. Retellings provide the teacher with a glimpse into student thinking. For example, Mr. Bradford asked Jasmine to retell a section of video clip they had seen related to glacier formation and movement. As part of her retelling, Jasmine said, "The glaciers take a long time to develop. Well, really they grow like something alive even though they're not alive. They develop when it snows and the snow piles together. It changes to this special kind of ice, but before that, there is this in-between ice called firn." This retelling lets Mr. Bradford know that much of his teaching has stuck and that Jasmine is well on her way to understanding glaciers.

Questioning

Questioning, which can be done orally or in writing, is the most common way that teachers check for understanding. Unfortunately, not all questions are worthy of instructional time. To be useful, the initial questions teachers ask should be planned in advance. Of course, additional questions that probe student understanding will come to mind during the interactions teachers have with students, but these initial questions form the expectations for student understanding. Less helpful questions are those we like to call "guess what's in the teacher's head." More formally known as Initiate–Respond–Evaluate or IRE (Cazden, 2001), this cycle privileges students who are willing to play the game. For example, when the teacher asks, "When do we use the FOIL rule?" Three or four students raise hands, and Tanya is selected to respond. Tanya says, "When you multiple binomials," to which the teacher responds, "Good." IRE is typically used with recall information and provides only a few students an opportunity to respond.

Instead, quality checking for understanding suggests that teachers need to ask questions that require more complex and critical thinking and that lots of students need to respond. There are a number of instructional routines that provide students with practice in questioning habits, such as ReQuest (Manzo, 1969), in which students read with a partner, taking turns asking and answering questions. As they practice, their teacher analyzes the types of questions being asked and the appropriateness of the answers. Over time (and with instruction and practice), students tire of the literal and recall questions and move toward more interesting questions that require synthesis and evaluation.

Another way to question in an inclusive way is through audience response systems. These can be as basic as 3- × 5-in. cards with answers on them that all students hold up to answer a question to as complex as handheld devices that allow each student to key in a response to a question. As an example of the former, as part of their opinionnaire in biology, students were provided with green and red cards, with *Yes* written on the green card and *No* written on the red card. As the teacher read each statement about the ecosystem, students held up one of their cards to indicate if they agreed or disagreed. A question about the impact of cleaning agents entering the water system through storm drains split the class, which provided the teacher information about where to focus the lesson. Audience responses systems, or "clickers," can be used to check for understanding of the whole class at once. For example, algebra teacher Aimee Chen poses a question and tells students to click in their responses and then invites them to persuade one another about their choice before revealing the answer. She then engages them in reteaching. There is now an online version of audience response systems that rely on text messages from cell phones that can be found at www.polleverywhere.com.

Writing

When students are writing, they are thinking. In fact, it's nearly impossible to write and *not* think. That's why short writing-to-learn prompts are so effective for checking for understanding. It's important that the prompt be developed such that it provides teachers with information about student understanding. We are particularly taken with the RAFT writing prompt (Santa & Havens, 1995), which requires that students consider the **r**ole, **a**udience, **f**ormat, and **t**opic in their writing. There are, of course, many other writing prompts that can be used, but RAFT is flexible and teaches perspective. For example, after discussing "being a good sport" in their physical education class, Mr. Davenport asks his students to respond to the following RAFT:

R   Bronze medal winner

A   Gold medal winner

F   Greeting card

T   Congratulations on your victory

Similarly, in a history classroom, students learn about the Gettysburg Address and discuss the role that this speech had in shaping U.S. policy. To check their understanding about the address, Ms. Ly asks her students to respond to the following RAFT:

R   person attending the Gettysburg dedication

A   family member

F   personal letter

T   Lincoln's message

Projects and Performances

On a larger scale, teachers can use projects and performances to check for understanding. Importantly, it is not done at the end when the project has been completed but rather as students work on these types of activities. There is a wide range of appropriate projects and performances that allow students an opportunity to engage in meaningful work aligned with content standards. As one example, Ms. Anderson's English class was focused on the essential question, "What's worth fighting, or even dying, for?" The students in this class wrote an essay in response to the question, read books such as *Romeo and Juliet*, and engaged in class debates. As one project, students created Facebook pages devoted to a worthy cause they

Video 6.3

Sample student debate.

resources.corwin.com/ rigorousreadingfla

would be willing to fight for. As they worked, Ms. Anderson viewed their pages in progress and met with individual students to check their understanding about the essential question. Micah created a page about CHARGE Syndrome, a rare genetic condition that his sister has. As he met with Ms. Anderson, Micah said, "I would fight for money to figure out what causes CHARGE and how to prevent it, I really would." Their discussion provided Ms. Anderson with evidence of Micah's developing understanding of worthy causes. Interestingly, Micah received a message on his Facebook cause page from a parent whose child with CHARGE Syndrome had died 17 years previously thanking him for his efforts.

Tests

Although tests are typically considered a summative assessment tool used for grading, they can also be used to check for understanding. Incorrect answers on a test provide teachers with information about what students still need to learn. Tests can be developed in a number of different formats, ranging from multiple choice to dichotomous choice (true/false, yes/no, agree/disagree) to essays. For example, on the following true/false question, 60% of the students answered incorrectly, informing their teacher that they are confused about some aspect of the life cycle of stars:

> As a star ages, its internal composition changes as nuclear reactions in the star's core convert one element into another.

Once the data are collected, teachers have to make decisions. The remainder of this chapter focuses on providing students feedback and making future instructional decisions based on the information.

▶ Providing Effective Feedback

Most of us have experienced poor feedback during our learning lives. The teacher who scrawled "rewrite this" in the margin of an essay we had written. The coach who told us, "No, you're doing it wrong, keep practicing." The coworker who took over the project and finished it for us when our progress stalled. The frustration on the learner's part matches that felt by the teacher, coach, or coworker: Why can't he or she get this? That mutual vexation produces a mutual sense of defeat. On the part of the learner, the internal dialogue becomes, "I can't do this." For the teacher, it's, "I can't teach this." Over time, blame sets in, and the student and teacher begin to find fault with each other.

Hattie and Timperley (2007) wrote about feedback across four dimensions: "Feedback about the task (FT), about the processing of the task (FP), about self-regulation (FR), and about the self as a person (FS)" (p. 90).

For example, "You need to put a semicolon in this sentence" (FT) has limited usefulness and is not usually generalized to other tasks.

On the other hand, "Make sure that your sentences have noun-verb agreements because it's going make it easier for the reader to understand your argument" (FP) gives feedback information about a writing convention necessary in all essays.

The researchers go on to note that feedback that moves from information about the process to information about self-regulation is the best of all. Such feedback might include something like the following: "Try reading some of your sentences aloud so you can hear when you have and don't have noun-verb agreement."

The researchers go on to say that FS is the least useful ("You're a good student") even when it is positive in nature because it doesn't add anything to one's learning. A summary of the types of feedback can be found in Figure 6.1.

The problem is that the task-related feedback offers only endgame analysis and leaves the learner with little direction on what to do, particularly when there isn't any recourse to make changes.

Done carefully, FT can have a modest amount of usefulness, as when editing a paper. Yet feedback about the task is by far the most common kind we offer. The problem is that the task-related feedback offers only endgame analysis and leaves the learner with little direction on what to do, particularly when there isn't any recourse to make changes. Most writing teachers will tell you that it is not uncommon for students to engage in limited revision, confined to the specific items listed in the teacher feedback—which then makes it more of an exercise in recopying than in revising. However, feedback about the processes used in the task, and further advice about the self-regulatory strategies one can use to make revisions, can leave the learner with a plan for next steps.

Consider the dialogue between English teacher Mark Harris and Alicia, a student in his class. Alicia has drafted an essay on bullying, and Mr. Harris is providing feedback about her work. Careful to frame his feedback so that it can result in a plan for revision, he draws her attention to her thesis statement and says, "It's helpful for writers to go back to the main point of the essay and read to see if the evidence is there. I highlight in yellow so I can see if I've done that." The two of them reread her first three paragraphs and highlight where she has provided national statistics and direct quotes from teachers she knows. "Now what I want you to do is to

Figure 6.1 Feedback Examples

Type	Example	Usefulness
Feedback about the task (FT)	"Make sure to change this from a period to an exclamation mark."	Limited
Feedback about the processing of the task (FP)	"You seem to want to emphasize this point. Be sure to use a strong verb to capture that intensity so your reader understands this as well."	Very useful
Feedback about self-regulation (FR)	"Read that passage aloud after you rewrite it to yourself to see if it matches the level of intensity you intend."	Very useful
Feedback about the self as a person (Fs)	"Good boy."	Not useful

look for ways you've provided supporting evidence, like through citing sources. Let's highlight those in green." Alicia quickly notices that while she has made claims, she hasn't capitalized on any authoritative sources. As well, by confining her direct quotes to teachers at her school, she has limited the impact of her essay by failing to quote more widely known sources. The little bit of green on her essay illustrates what she needs to do next: strengthen her sources. "It sounds like you have a plan for revising the content. Let's meet again on Wednesday and you can update me on your progress."

Feedback of this nature takes a few minutes yet can add up quickly in a crowded classroom. For this reason, many teachers rely on written forms of feedback as a substitute for direct conversations. Even when providing feedback in written form, the guidelines described above remain the same: Focus on the processes needed for the task, move to information about behaviors that are within the student's influence to change, and steer clear of comments that are either too global or too minute to be of much use. Wiggins (1998) advises constructing written feedback so that it meets four important criteria. First, it must be timely so that it is paired as closely as possible with the attempt; second, it should be specific in nature; third, it should be written in a manner that it understandable to the student; and fourth, it should be actionable so that the learner can make revisions.

While feedback is primarily offered at the individual level, the concept of feeding-up refers to the process of making instructional decisions about what should happen next for the class as a whole.

▶ Engaging in Feed-Forward Instruction

While feedback is primarily offered at the individual level, the concept of *feeding-up* refers to the process of making instructional decisions about what should happen next for the class as a whole (Frey & Fisher, 2011). Data about student progress are commonly gathered using common formative assessments that are either commercially produced or teacher-made. In addition, many school teams engage in consensus scoring with colleagues to calibrate assessment practices, especially those associated with tasks that have a significant qualitative component, such as writing (Fisher, Frey, Farnan, Fearn, & Petersen, 2004). However, consensus scoring requires time for colleagues to work together—something that can be hard to come by and can therefore be a limitation to these practices. The good news is that one's own classroom can also serve as the unit of analysis for formative assessment.

With all of the solid feedback provided to students, it seems natural to take this one step further by recording results and doing some pattern analysis. For example, second-grade teacher Elena Vitsen conferred with students during their independent reading to check on their progress toward meeting the standard that students "explain how text features—including titles, headings, captions, graphs, maps, glossaries, and/or illustrations—contribute to the meaning of texts" (Florida Department of Education, 2020, p. 44).

"I've been working with them on how we use images, captions, and subheadings to scan and locate information in texts," she explained. "I've been checking in with them about using their science textbook this way." She selects an unfamiliar passage from the book and asks questions about the content of the caption and image, as well as its relation to the main portion of the text. "I'm especially interested right now in whether they are able to accurately predict the content of the passage and figure out where the image belongs," she said. Her error analysis sheet is in Figure 6.2.

Unlike a checklist to track mastery, this error analysis sheet is used to identify and highlight those who are struggling. She logs the initials of students who are still having difficulty with major concepts despite initial instruction, then makes decisions about follow-up and reteaching. For example, the error analysis sheet showed her that almost the entire class was still having difficulty relating the visual to the correct passage. That tells her that reteaching to the whole group is in order. On the other hand, smaller groups of students were having trouble with other concepts:

> I was surprised that I still had a few who aren't using bold words effectively. We've had lots of experiences with these, and I thought everyone had it. I'll need to pull those students into a small group, because the majority of the class is doing fine otherwise.

She will plan further scaffolded instruction for these small groups.

Seventh-grade English teacher Kari McGee is also concerned with examining her students' progress toward informational reading, specifically the expectation that students "track the development of an argument, analyzing the types of reasoning used and their effectiveness." Ms. McGee has taught her students the types of reasoning identified in the Florida standards (see Figure 6.3). Before focusing on the fallacies in reasoning, Ms. McGee assessed her students' knowledge to determine gaps in their understanding. She provided students with passages of text and asked them to identify the type of reasoning used. As she said, "If students can't identify the types of reasoning, then they won't be able to track the development of an argument and think about the effectiveness of the reasoning."

Consensus scoring requires time for colleagues to work together—something that can be hard to come by and can therefore be a limitation to these practices.

Video 6.4

Daily checks for understanding help teachers identify instructional needs.
resources.corwin.com/ rigorousreadingfla

Video 6.5

Teacher discusses his use of error analysis.
resources.corwin.com/ rigorousreadingfla

Figure 6.2   Grade 2 Error Analysis of Print and Graphic Features

Task	Initials of Students Who Are Having Difficulty With This Skill
Locates caption	
Reads caption and relates it to the text	
Reads caption and relates it to the visual information	
Locates bold word	
Describes the role of bold words	
Finds meaning of bold word using glossary	
Locates subheading	
Describes content expected in the section based on the subheading	
Identifies appropriate visual/graphic and caption related to the text in a subheading	

Figure 6.3 Types of Logical Reasoning

Deductive	Inductive	Abductive
Characteristics		
• Begins with a premise • Uses a given fact or set of facts to deduce other facts • Does not provide new information • Follows a pattern: "If this is true, then this is also true" • Begins with the general and moves to the specific	• Begins with a specific observation and applies to a broad conclusion	• Begins with a pattern or a trend • Uses a pattern to extrapolate information consistent with the given pattern • Begins with the specific and moves to generalize
Examples		
Premise: Whales are mammals. **Fact:** Orcas are a type of whale. **Conclusion:** Orcas are mammals.	**Observation:** The bakery across the street always has a line out the door. **Conclusion:** The bakery sells delicious treats.	**Pattern:** My grandparents all have grey hair. **Conclusion:** All elderly people have grey hair.

Source: Florida Department of Education (2020, p. 180).

Ms. McGee created an error analysis tool that allowed her to identify the patterns of errors her students made (see Figure 6.4). She noted that across all of her classes, students were more likely to indicate that the reasoning was deductive. They rarely said that it was abductive. She also noted that period 3 struggled the most and that over half of the students had errors in identifying reasoning. As she said, "I need to reteach the differences in reasoning and have them practice this again. And I need to pay special attention to third period as they are really struggling with this topic." Ms. McGee also noted that several students answered incorrectly on almost all of the questions, and she decided that she would meet with them for additional small-group instruction.

Ms. Schamberg developed a different error analysis tool for her fourth graders. Rather than examine the whole class at the same time, she created an error analysis sheet for each student to focus on their verb usage (see Figure 6.5). In this case, Ms. Schamberg reviewed a timed writing sample and analyzed the number of attempts for each item, such as simple present tense or simple past tense with -*ed*. She calculated the number of times

Figure 6.4 Error Analysis for Logical Reasoning

Error	Period 1	Period 2	Period 3	Period 4	Period 5
Indicated deductive but was inductive					
Indicated deductive but was abductive					
Indicated inductive but was deductive					
Indicated inductive but was abductive					
Indicated abductive but was deductive					
Indicated abductive but was inductive					
No reasoning was identified					

Figure 6.5 Fourth-Grade Verb Usage

Verb Form	Total Attempts	Correct Usage	Errors	Percentage of Errors
Student's writing displays subject–verb agreement				
Student utilizes the simple present tense				
Student utilizes simple past tense with -ed				
Student utilizes simple future tense with the helping verb will				
Student uses the present perfect tense with the helping verbs has and have				
Student uses the past perfect tense with the helping verb had				
Student demonstrates the ability to write the "be" verbs is, am, are, was, and were with singular and plural nouns				

Video 6.6

Teacher reteaches students to use evidence after the error analysis revealed a need.

resources.corwin.com/ rigorousreadingfla

a student did it correctly and how often they made errors on a given verb usage. This allowed her to calculate the percentage of errors for each item. As she noted, "I don't just want to record the errors. I want to see if the frequency of errors is reducing. I need to analyze this for each individual student and then form groups to address the gaps that I see in their understanding. These tools allow me to be much more diagnostic and really drill down to the areas that require more attention."

▶ Summary

We are changed by text. We use complex texts to bring the world into our classrooms. But students' potential for learning remains untapped until we provide them with culminating assessments that are equally as complex as the texts they are reading. The texts you choose should serve as a platform for extending ideas and building curiosity. But how do you know if students understand the texts they are reading, or if they need additional information? Through careful observation. What we hear students say during discussion, or read in their writing, sparks further understanding about what should come next. In this way, student assessment never ends until the very last day of school. Caring teachers apply what they have learned about their students to future instruction. They use feedback in ways that build student understanding, and they look for the patterns that will inform their next instructional moves. It is much in the manner of the sheep tender looking over the flock. According to Brick (1908),

> The man who does not like sheep, and who is not willing to devote lots of time to their care . . . has no business meddling with the Spring Lamb . . . To be successful, he must also be gentle, with a watchful eye for little things . . . and a hundred minor details upon which success depends. (p. 154)

In short, the tender must also heed the warning Brick delivered almost a century ago: "You can't fatten sheep by weighing them." In the same way, it is through nurturing and feeding our students—and not merely through measuring them—that we provide them with a window through which they can see the world and themselves in the words of others.

Video 6.7

Nancy leads a group of teachers in a data review.

resources.corwin.com/ rigorousreadingfla

Coda

We have come to the end of this book with just a few words left before you close the cover. You have read this book because you care deeply about your craft and your students. We applaud you for that. You know that simply assigning students complex texts and then wishing them well is not going to yield breakthrough results. You also know that teaching is more than test scores. Yes, providing students access to complex texts will improve their achievement on the next generation of assessments. But more than that, accessing complex texts invites students into the scholarly world. This may sound like hyperbole, but we really believe that unlocking complex texts is the most important thing a teacher can do for his or her students. And now that you have read this book, you have the keys in your hands. The access points in this book work. They ensure that students have the experiences, instruction, and support necessary to read and understand the wide range of texts they will encounter throughout their lives.

References

Adler, M. J., & Van Doren, C. (1972). *How to read a book*. New York: Touchstone.

Afflerbach, P., Pearson, P. D., & Paris, S. G. (2008). Clarifying differences between reading skills and reading strategies. *The Reading Teacher, 61*(5), 364–373.

Alexander, P. A., & Jetton, T. L. (2000). Learning from text: A multidimensional and developmental perspective. In M. L. Kamil, P. B. Mosenthal, P. D. Pearson, & R. Barr (Eds.), *Handbook of reading research* (Vol. 3, pp. 285–310). Mahwah, NJ: Erlbaum.

Allington, R. L. (2002). You can't learn much from books you can't read. *Educational Leadership, 60*(3), 16–19.

Anderson, L., Brubaker, N., Alleman-Brooks, J., & Duffy, G. (1985). A qualitative study of seatwork in first-grade classrooms. *Elementary School Journal, 86*, 123–140.

Anderson, R. C., Wilson, P. T., & Fielding, L. G. (1988). Growth in reading and how children spend their time outside school. *Reading Research Quarterly, 23*, 285–303.

Avalos, M. A., Plasencia, A., Chavez, C., & Rascón, J. (2007/2008). Modified guided reading: Gateway to English as a second language and literacy learning. *The Reading Teacher, 61*, 318–329.

Banks, J. A., & Banks, C. A. M. (2012). *Multicultural education: Issues and perspectives* (8th ed.). New York: Wiley.

Baum, L. F. (1900/2000). *The wonderful wizard of Oz*. New York: HarperCollins.

Becklake, S. (1998). *All about space*. New York, NY: Scholastic.

Bennett, N., & Cass, A. (1989). The effects of group composition on group interactive processes and pupil understanding. *British Educational Research Journal, 15*(1), 19–32.

Biemiller, A. (2003). Oral comprehension sets the ceiling on reading comprehension. *American Educator*. Retrieved from https://www.aft.org/periodical/american-educator/spring-2003/oral-comprehension-sets-ceiling-reading

Bonsignore, J. (2001). *Stick out your tongue! Fantastic facts, features, and functions of animal and human tongues*. Atlanta, GA: Peachtree.

Brick, H. (1908). Early spring lambs. *The Farm Journal, 32*(4), 153–154.

Britton, J. (1970). *Language and learning.* Coral Gables, FL: University of Miami.

Bromley, K. D. (1985). Précis writing and outlining to enhance content learning. *The Reading Teacher, 38*(4), 406–411.

Brown, A. L., & Day, J. D. (1983). Macrorules for summarizing texts: The development of expertise. *Journal of Verbal Learning and Verbal Behavior, 22,* 1–14.

Buehl, D. (2009). *Classroom strategies for interactive learning* (3rd ed.). Newark, DE: International Reading Association.

Campbell, J. R., Voelkl, K. E., & Donahue, P. L. (1997). *NAEP 1996 trends in academic progress* (Report No. NCES-97-986). Princeton, NJ: National Assessment of Educational Progress. (ERIC Document Reproduction Service No. ED411327)

Carle, E. (1996). *The grouchy ladybug.* New York: HarperCollins.

Carroll, C. (1997). *How artists see families.* New York: Abbeville Kids.

Cazden, C. B. (2001). *Classroom discourse: The language of teaching and learning.* Portsmouth, NH: Heinemann.

Cisneros, S. (1991). *Woman hollering creek, and other stories.* New York: Random House.

Clay, M. M. (2001). *Change over time in children's literacy development.* Portsmouth, NH: Heinemann.

Clements, A. (1996). *Frindle.* New York: Aladdin.

Daniels, H. (2002). *Literature circles: Voice and choice in book clubs and reading groups* (2nd ed.). York, ME: Stenhouse.

Davey, B. (1983). Think aloud: Modeling the cognitive processes for reading comprehension. *Journal of Reading, 27,* 44–47.

Dean, C. B., Stone, B. J., Hubbell, E., & Pitler, H. (2012). *Classroom instruction that works: Research-based strategies for increasing student achievement* (2nd ed.). Alexandria, VA: ASCD.

Donovan, M. S., & Bransford, J. D. (Eds.). (2005). *How students learn: Science in the classroom.* Washington, DC: National Academies Press.

Duffy, G. G. (2014). *Explaining reading: A resource for teaching concepts, skills, and strategies* (3rd ed.). New York: Guilford.

Elbaum, B., Schumm, J. S., & Vaughn, S. (1997). Urban middle-elementary students' perceptions of grouping formats for reading instruction. *Elementary School Journal, 97,* 475–500.

Elley, W. B. (2000). The potential of book floods for raising literary levels. *International Review of Education, 46*(3–4), 233–255.

Evans, L. (2011). *Moon power.* New York, NY: Scholastic.

Fang, Z. (2012). Approaches to developing content area literacies: A synthesis and critique. *Journal of Adolescent & Adult Literacy, 56*(2), 103–108.

Faust, M. A., & Glenzer, N. (2000). "I could read those parts over and over": Eighth graders rereading to enhance enjoyment and learning with literature. *Journal of Adolescent & Adult Literacy, 44,* 234–239.

Fisher, D., Flood, J., Lapp, D., & Frey, N. (2004). Interactive read alouds: Is there a common set of implementation practices? *The Reading Teacher, 58,* 8–17.

Fisher, D., & Frey, N. (2008). *Better learning for structured teaching: A framework for the gradual release of responsibility.* Alexandria, VA: ASCD.

Fisher, D., & Frey, N. (2010a). *Enhancing RTI: How to ensure success with effective classroom instruction and intervention.* Alexandria, VA: ASCD.

Fisher, D., & Frey, N. (2010b). *Guided instruction: How to develop confident and successful learners.* Alexandria, VA: ASCD.

Fisher, D., & Frey, N. (2012a). Close reading in elementary schools. *The Reading Teacher, 66,* 179–188.

Fisher, D., & Frey, N. (2012b). *Improving adolescent literacy: Content area strategies at work* (3rd ed.). Boston: Allyn & Bacon.

Fisher, D., & Frey, N. (2013a). *Better learning through structured teaching: A framework for the gradual release of responsibility* (2nd ed.). Alexandria, VA: ASCD.

Fisher, D., & Frey, N. (2013b). *Common Core English language arts in a PLC at work: Grades 3–5.* Bloomington, IN: Solution Tree.

Fisher, D., & Frey, N. (2014). *Checking for understanding: Formative assessment techniques for your classroom* (2nd ed.). Alexandria, VA: ASCD.

Fisher, D., Frey, N., Farnan, N., Fearn, L., & Petersen, F. (2004). Increasing writing achievement in an urban middle school. *Middle School Journal, 36*(2), 21–26.

Fisher, D., Frey, N., & Hattie, J. (2016). *Visible learning for literacy: Implementing the practices that work best to accelerate student learning.* Thousand Oaks, CA: Corwin.

Fisher, D., Frey, N., & Lapp, D. (2008). *In a reading state of mind: Brain research, teacher modeling, and comprehension instruction.* Newark, DE: International Reading Association.

Fisher, D., Frey, N., & Lapp, D. (2016). *Text complexity: Stretching readers with texts and tasks.* Thousand Oaks, CA: Corwin.

Fisher, D., Frey, N., & Rothenberg, C. (2008). *Content area conversations: How to plan discussion-based lessons for diverse language learners.* Alexandria, VA: ASCD.

Fisher, D., Lapp, D., & Frey, N. (2011). Comprehension: The cooperation of many forces. In D. Lapp & D. Fisher (Eds.), *Handbook of research on teaching the English language arts* (3rd ed.) (pp. 258–263). New York: Routledge.

Fisher, D., McDonald, N. L., & Frey, N. (2013). Integration of literacy and the arts: Creating classrooms that perform. In B. Taylor & N. Duke (Eds.), *Effective literacy instruction: A handbook of research and practice* (pp. 446–464). New York, NY: Guilford.

Fisher, D., Ross, D., & Grant, M. (2010). Building background knowledge in physical science. *The Science Teacher, 77*(1), 23–26.

Fleischman, P. (2006). *Dateline: Troy.* Somerville, MA: Candlewick.

Florida Department of Education. (2020). *Florida's B.E.S.T. Standards: English language arts.* Retrieved from http://www.fldoe.org/core/fileparse.php/18736/urlt/ELAStandards.PDF

Fountas, I., & Pinnell, G. (2012). Guided reading: The romance and the reality. *The Reading Teacher, 66*(4), 268–284.

Frey, N., & Fisher, D. (2010). Identifying instructional moves during guided learning. *The Reading Teacher, 64*(2), 84–95.

Frey, N., & Fisher, D. (2011). *The formative assessment action plan: Practical steps to more successful teaching and learning.* Alexandria, VA: ASCD.

Frey, N., Fisher, D., & Everlove, S. (2009). *Productive group work: How to engage students, build teamwork, and promote understanding.* Alexandria, VA: ASCD.

Gibbons, G. (1993). *From seed to plant.* New York, NY: Holiday House.

Gibson, F. (1956). *Old Yeller.* New York: HarperCollins.

Good, T. L., & Brophy, J. E. (2003). *Looking in classrooms* (9th ed.). Boston: Allyn & Bacon.

Graff, G., & Birkenstein, C. (2006). *They say / I say: The moves that matter in academic writing.* New York: W. W. Norton & Company.

Gregory, K. (2001). *Seeds of hope: The gold rush diary of Susanna Fairchild (Dear America).* New York: Scholastic.

Guthrie, J. T., Hoa, A.L.W., Wigfield, A., Tonks, S. M., Humenick, N. M., & Littles, E. (2007). Reading motivation and reading comprehension growth in the later elementary years. *Contemporary Educational Psychology, 32*(3), 282–313.

Guthrie, J. T., Schafer, W. D., & Huang, C. (2001). Benefits of opportunity to read and balanced instruction on the NAEP. *Journal of Educational Research, 94,* 145–162.

Guthrie, J. T., & Wigfield, A. (2000). Engagement and motivation in reading. In M. L. Kamil, P. B. Mosenthal, P. D. Pearson, & R. Barr (Eds.), *Handbook of reading research* (Vol. 3, pp. 403–424). Mahwah, NJ: Erlbaum.

Harvey, V. S., & Chickie-Wolf, L. A. (2007). *Fostering independent learning: Practical strategies to promote student success.* New York: Guilford.

Hattie, J., & Timperley, H. (2007). The power of feedback. *Review of Educational Research, 77,* 81–112.

Hattie, J. A. C., & Donoghue, G. M. (2016). Learning strategies: A synthesis and conceptual model. *Science of Learning, 1.* doi:10.1038/npjscilearn2016.

Hesse, K. (1996). *The music of dolphins*. New York: Scholastic.

Hiebert, E. H. (Ed.). (2009). *Reading more, reading better: Solving problems in the teaching of literacy*. New York: Guilford.

Hill, J. D., & Flynn, K. M. (2006). *Classroom instruction that works with English language learners*. Alexandria, VA: Association for Supervision and Curriculum Development.

Holdaway, D. (1979). *The foundations of literacy*. Portsmouth, NH: Heinemann.

Hua, W., Cromwell, A. M., & McClarty, K. L. (2016). Career readiness: An analysis of text complexity for occupational reading materials. *Journal of Educational Research, 109*(3), 266–274.

Hudson, A. (2016). Get them talking! Using student-led book talks in the primary grades. *The Reading Teacher, 70*(2), 221–225.

Hulit, L. M., Howard, M. R., & Fahey, K. R. (2010). *Born to talk: An introduction to speech and language development*. Boston, MA: Allyn & Bacon.

Hunter, M. C. (1976). *Improved instruction*. Thousand Oaks, CA: Corwin.

Iowa State University. (2007, May 31). Psychologist explains teens' risky decision-making behavior. *ScienceDaily*. Retrieved from http://www.sciencedaily.com/releases/2007/05/070531093830.htm

Johnson, D. W., Johnson, R. T., & Holubec, E. J. (2008). *Cooperation in the classroom* (8th ed.). Edina, MN: Interaction.

Johnson, D., Johnson, R., Holubec, E. J., & Roy, P. (1984). *Circles of learning: Cooperation in the classroom*. Alexandria, VA: ASCD.

Kafka, F. (1946). *Metamorphosis*. New York: Vanguard Press.

Kapur, M. (2008). Productive failure. *Cognition and Instruction, 26*(3), 379–424.

Klinger, J. K., & Vaughn, S. (1998). Using collaborative strategic reading. *TEACHING Exceptional Children, 30*(6), 32–37.

Klinger, J. K., Vaughn, S., & Schumm, J. S. (1998). Collaborative strategic reading during social studies in heterogeneous fourth-grade classrooms. *Elementary School Journal, 99*, 3–20.

Kush, J. C., & Watkins, M. W. (1996). Long-term stability of children's attitudes toward reading. *Journal of Educational Research, 89*, 315–319.

Lobel, A. (1971). *Frog and toad together*. New York: HarperCollins.

Lord, W. (1955). *A night to remember*. New York: St. Martin's Griffin.

Lowry, L. (1989). *Number the stars*. New York: Laurel Leaf.

Manzo, A. (1969). ReQuest: A method for improving reading comprehension through reciprocal questioning. *Journal of Reading, 12*, 123–126.

Marinak, B. A., & Gambrell, L. B. (2016). *No more reading for junk: Best practices for motivating readers.* Portsmouth, NH: Heinemann.

Marzano, R. J. (2009). *Designing & teaching learning goals and objectives.* Bloomington, IN: Solution Tree.

Marzano, R. J., Pickering, D. J., & Pollock, J. E. (2002). *Classroom instruction that works: Research-based strategies for increasing student achievement.* Alexandria, VA: Association for Supervision and Curriculum Development.

Matthews, M. W., & Kesner, J. (2003). Children learning with peers: The confluence of peer status and literacy competence within small-group literacy events. *Reading Research Quarterly, 38,* 208–234.

McLaughlin, M., & DeVoogd, G. L. (2004). *Critical literacy: Enhancing students' comprehension of text.* New York: Scholastic.

Millis, K. K., & King, A. (2001). Rereading strategically: The influences of comprehension ability and a prior reading on the memory for expository text. *Reading Psychology, 22,* 41–65.

National Governors Association. (2010). *Common Core State Standards for English language arts and literacy in history/social studies, science and technical subjects. Appendix A: research supporting key elements of the standards.* Retrieved at http://www.corestandards.org/assets/Appendix_A.pdf

Neuman, S. (2017). The information book flood: Is additional exposure enough to support early literacy development? *The Elementary School Journal, 118*(1), 1–27.

Newman, P. (2014). *Plastic, ahoy!: Investigating the great Pacific garbage patch.* Minneapolis, MN: Millbrook.

Newkirk, T. (2010). The case for slow reading. *Educational Leadership, 67*(6), 6–11.

Nystrand, M., & Gamoran, A. (1991). Instructional discourse, student engagement, and literature achievement. *Research in the Teaching of English, 25,* 261–290.

Optiz, M. F., & Rasinski, T. V. (2008). *Good-bye round robin: 25 effective oral reading strategies* (updated ed.). Portsmouth, NH: Heinemann.

Palincsar, A. S., & Brown, A. L. (1984). Reciprocal teaching of comprehension-fostering and comprehension-monitoring activities. *Cognition and Instruction, 1*(2), 117–175.

Pearson, P. D., & Fielding, L. (1991). Comprehension instruction. In R. Barr, M. L. Kamil, P. Mosenthal, & P. D. Pearson (Eds.), *Handbook of reading research* (Vol. 2, pp. 815–860). Mahwah, NJ: Erlbaum.

Pearson, P. D., & Gallagher, M. C. (1983). The instruction of reading comprehension. *Contemporary Educational Psychology, 8,* 317–344.

Pinkney, J. (2009). *The lion and the mouse.* New York: Little, Brown.

Pinnell, G. S., & Fountas, I. C. (2003). Teaching comprehension. *The California Reader, 36*(4), 7–14.

Pressley, M., El-Dinary, P. B., Gaskins, I., Schuder, T., Bergman, J. L., Almasi, J., et al. (1992). Beyond direct explanation: Transactional instruction of reading comprehension strategies. *The Elementary School Journal, 92,* 513–555.

Richards, I. A. (1929). *Practical criticism.* London: Cambridge University Press.

Rog, L. J. (2001). *Early literacy instruction in kindergarten.* Newark, DE: International Reading Association.

Rosenblatt, L. M. (1938/1995). *Literature as exploration* (5th ed.). New York: Modern Language Association.

Rosenblatt, L. M. (2003). Literary theory. In J. Flood, D. Lapp, J. R. Squire, & J. M. Jensen (Eds.), *Handbook of research on teaching the English language arts* (pp. 67–73). New York: Macmillan.

Ryan, P. M. (1999). *Riding freedom.* New York: Scholastic.

Santa, C. M, & Havens, L. T. (1995). *Project CRISS: Creating independence through student-owned strategies.* Dubuque, IA: Kendall/Hunt.

Santa, C., & Havens, L. (1995). *Creating independence through student-owned strategies: Project CRISS.* Dubuque, IA: Kendall Hunt.

Schunk, D. H. (1998). Goal and self-evaluative influences during children's cognitive skill learning. *American Educational Research Journal, 33,* 359–382.

Schunk, D. H., Meece, J. R., & Pintrich, P. R. (2013). *Motivation in education: Theory, research, and applications* (4th ed.). Boston, MA: Pearson.

Sendak, M. (1963). *Where the wild things are.* New York: Harper & Rowe.

Skouge, J. R., Rao, K., & Boisvert, P. C. (2007). Promoting early literacy for diverse learners using audio and video technology. *Early Childhood Education Journal, 35*(1), 5–11.

Smith, M. C. (1950, June 1). *Declaration of conscience.* US Congress, Senate, Congressional Record, 81st Congress, 2d sess., 7894–7895. Retrieved from http://www.americanrhetoric.com/speeches/margaretchasesmithconscience.html

Smith, M. C. (2000). The real-world reading practices of adults. *Journal of Literacy Research, 32,* 25–52.

Spinelli, J. (2003). *Stargirl.* New York: Scholastic.

Stanovich, K. E. (1986). Matthew effects in reading: Some consequences of individual differences in the acquisition of literacy. *Reading Research Quarterly, 21,* 360–407.

Steinbeck, J. (1945). *The pearl.* New York: Penguin Books.

Stricht, T. G., & James, J. H. (1984). Listening and reading. In P. D. Pearson, R. Barr, M. L. Kamil, & P. Mosenthal (Eds.), *Handbook of reading research* (Vol. 1, pp. 293–317). White Plains, NY: Longman.

Stright, A. D., & Supplee, L. H. (2002). Children's self-regulatory behaviors during teacher-directed, seat-work, and small-group instructional contexts. *Journal of Educational Research, 95,* 235–246.

Tatham, B. (2002). *How animals shed their skin.* New York: Franklin Watts.

Tayback, S. (1999). *Joseph had a little overcoat.* New York: Viking.

Tayback, S. (2007). *There was an old lady who swallowed a fly.* Auburn, ME: Child's Play International.

Trivizas, E. (1993). *The three little wolves and the big bad pig.* New York: Aladdin.

Vygotsky, L. S. (1978). *Mind in society: The development of higher psychological processes* (M. Cole, V. John-Steiner, S. Scribner, & E. Souberman, Eds. & Trans.). Cambridge, MA: Harvard University Press.

Weber, K. (Ed.). (2012). *Last call at the oasis: The global water crisis and where we go from here.* New York: PublicAffairs.

Wiesel, E. (1982). *Night.* New York: Bantam.

Wiggins, G. (1998). *Educative assessment: Designing assessments to inform and improve student performance.* San Francisco: Jossey-Bass.

Wiggins, G., & McTighe, J. (2005). *Understanding by design* (2nd ed.). Alexandria, VA: ASCD.

Wilhelm, J. D. (2001). Think-alouds boost reading comprehension. *Instructor, 111*(4), 26–28.

Winter, J. (2002). *Frida.* New York: Arthur A. Levine.

Wolf, M. (2007). *Proust and the squid: The story and science of the reading brain.* New York, NY: HarperCollins.

Wood, A. (2009). *The napping house.* San Diego: Harcourt Brace.

Wood, D., Bruner, J. S., & Ross, G. (1976). The role of tutoring in problem solving. *Journal of Child Psychology and Psychiatry, 17*(2), 89–100.

Wood, D., & Wood, H. (1996). Vygotsky, tutoring and learning. *Oxford Review of Education, 22*(1), 5–16.

Wozniak, C. L. (2011). Reading and talking about books: A critical foundation for intervention. *Voices From the Middle, 19*(2), 17–21.

Yeager, D., & Dweck, C. (2012). Mindsets that promote resilience: When students believe that personal characteristics can be developed. *Educational Psychologist, 47*(4), 302–314.

Young, C., & Rasinski, T. (2009). Implementing readers theatre as an approach to classroom fluency instruction. *The Reading Teacher, 63*(1), 4–13.

Index

teacher-directed groups in, 87
whole-class, trouble with, 76–77
Schumm, J. S., 87
Secret Garden, The, 2
Self-assessment, 91, 92 (figure),
   93 (figure)
Self-regulation in independent
   learning, 107
Shared readings, 35–38
Small groups in scaffolded reading
   instruction, 70
Smith, M. C., 49
Social learning intentions, 41,
   41 (figure)
Stanovich, K. E., 110
Stargirl, 68
Stick Out Your Tongue!, 97–98
Sticky notes, 114
"Stopping by Woods on a Snowy
   Evening," 117
Storybird, 100
Storytelling, digital, 100–101
Stricht, T. G., 81
Stright, A. D., 107
Structural analysis of words,
   29–30
Structural questions, 54 (figure), 56
   author's craft and purpose,
      55 (figure), 58, 61, 64
   vocabulary and text structure,
      55 (figure), 57–58, 61, 64
Student-centered considerations, text
   complexity, 7–9, 9 (figure)
Summarizing, 96–97
Supplee, L. H., 107
Sustained silent reading (SSR),
   112–114, 113 (figure)

Targas, Lisa, 118–119
Tests, 132
Text complexity. *See* Complex texts
Text-dependent questions, 51–60,
   54 (figure), 55 (figure), 61, 64
   author's craft and purpose, 58
   general understandings, 56–57
   inferences, 59
   inferential level of, 54 (figure), 56
   key details, 57
   literal level of, 53, 54 (figure), 56
   opinions, arguments, and
      intertextual connections,
      59–60

structural level of, 54 (figure), 56
vocabulary and text structure,
   57–58
*There Was an Old Lady Who Swallowed
   a Fly*, 119
Think-aloud, 22–23, 33–35
   effective, 34 (figure)
   during shared reading, 37–38
*Three Little Wolves and the Big Bad Pig,
   The*, 27–28
Timer in CSR, 97
Timperley, H., 133
Tomás Rivera award, 8

Upper grades, close reading in,
   65 (figure)

Vaca, Javier, 94
Van Doren, C., 31
Vaughn, S., 87
Verbal cues, 75 (figure)
Visual cues, 75 (figure)
Vitsen, Elena, 135
Vocabulary and text structure questions,
   55 (figure), 57–58, 61, 64
Vocabulary strand, B.E.S.T.
   Standards, 15
VoiceThread, 100–101

Washington, George, 50
"Way Forward? The Soft Path for
   Water, A," 52–53
Where the Wild Things Are, 37
Wiggins, G., 135
Wilhelm, J. D., 23
Wonderful Wizard of Oz, The, 63
Words
   context clues of, 30
   morphology, 29
   structural analysis of, 29–30
   using resources to look up,
      30–31
Work-avoidant goals, 108
Wozniak, C. L., 122
Wrap up, reading, 97–101
Writing in checking for
   understanding, 131
Writing-to-learn prompts, 131
Wyatt, Thomas, 50–51

Young readers, close reading for,
   63–66

CORWIN Fisher & Frey

" Every student deserves a great
teacher—not by chance, but by design. "

Read more from Fisher & Frey

DOUGLAS FISHER, NANCY FREY, NANCY AKHAVAN

Tap your intuition, collaborate with your peers, and put the research-based strategies embedded in this roadmap to work in your classroom to implement or deepen a strong, successful balanced literacy program.

DOUGLAS FISHER, NANCY FREY, OLIVIA AMADOR, JOSEPH ASSOF

With cross-curricular examples, planning templates, professional learning questions, and a PLC guide, this is the most practical planner for designing and delivering highly effective instruction.

DOUGLAS FISHER, NANCY FREY, RUSSELL J. QUAGLIA, DOMINIQUE SMITH, LISA L. LANDE

Engagement by Design puts you in control of managing your classroom's success and increasing student learning, one motivated student at a time.

DOUGLAS FISHER, NANCY FREY, DIANE LAPP

In this edition of the best-selling *Text Complexity,* the renowned author team lays open the instructional routines that take students to new places as readers.

DOUGLAS FISHER, NANCY FREY

Nancy Frey and Douglas Fisher articulate an instructional plan for close reading so clearly and so squarely built on research that it's the only resource a teacher will need.

DOUGLAS FISHER, NANCY FREY, HEATHER ANDERSON, MARISOL THAYRE

The authors break down the process into four cognitive pathways that help teachers "organize the journey through a text" and frame an extended discussion around it.

To order your copies, visit corwin.com/FisherandFrey

A SAGE Publishing Company

Helping educators make the greatest impact

CORWIN HAS ONE MISSION: to enhance education through intentional professional learning.

We build long-term relationships with our authors, educators, clients, and associations who partner with us to develop and continuously improve the best evidence-based practices that establish and support lifelong learning.